FISHING
CANADA'S MOUNTAIN PARKS

Also available in the
LONE PINE Outdoor Series:

The Northern Naturalist
Bicycle Alberta
Ski Alberta
The Canadian Ice Angler's Guide
Canoeing Alberta
The Canadian Rockies Access Guide
Camping Alberta
The Complete Guide to Kananaskis Country

FISHING
CANADA'S MOUNTAIN PARKS

James R. Butler and Roland R. Maw

The Publishers:
Lone Pine Publishing
Edmonton, Alberta

Typeset in Clearface and Futura by Pièce de Résistance Typographers, Edmonton

Printed by Commercial Color Press Ltd., Edmonton

Canadian Cataloguing in Publication Data

Butler, James R.
  Fishing Canada's mountain parks

Includes index.
ISBN 0-919433-43-X

1. Fishing–Canada, Western. 2. Parks—Canada, Western. 3. Fishes, Fresh-water—Canada, Western. I. Maw, Roland R. II. Title.

Front cover photo: courtesy Alberta Fish & Wildlife
Back cover photo: John Denengelsen
Cover design: Sharon McIntyre
Book design: Allan Shute and Mark Giles
Layout: Sharon McIntyre and Jaime Romero
Map: Jaime Romero
Illustrations: David Marko and Jaime Romero

ACKNOWLEDGEMENTS

The authors wish to express their gratitude and appreciation to a large number of people and organizations who assisted in various ways.

The Waterton Natural History Association provided a grant for the cost of typing and assembling the photos. Partial funding was also provided through a contribution to the publishing program of the Waterton Lakes Natural History Association, making possible the extensive number of color photos used in this publication. Lone Pine Publishing offered encouragement and made it financially possible to extensively enlarge the book.

We are especially grateful to Wayne Roberts, curator of the University of Alberta Museum of Zoology, for his review of the manuscript and helpful advice and suggestions. David B. Donald of the Canadian Wildlife Service provided extensive background information from his research work in the national parks, from which we borrowed freely. Dr. Leon Carl of the Alberta Fish and Wildlife Division contributed much helpful information. Dana Dolsen reviewed and contributed to the section on catch-and-release fishing. Bob Purdy and Elaine Butler provided some of the specialized photography. Duane Barrus, Ken Goble, Dr. Bernie Lieff, and Max Winkler from Waterton Lakes National Park and Dr. Keith Shaw provided a review of the manuscript and helpful advice. Special thanks to Joy Lieff, business manager for the Waterton Natural History Association, for her patience and encouragement.

Both authors also involved students from their relevant educational institutions in this project, and their contributions are sincerely appreciated. These students included, at the University of Alberta, Dana Dolsen, Bob Purdy, Sue Ellen Fast, Glen Wonders, Murray Fowler, Brent Rabik, Heather Pritchard, Terry Kuzma, Michael Kelly, Billy Hoskin, Art Meyers, Mark Messmer, Dave Pinnel and Barry Mills. Students who assisted the project at Lethbridge Community College include Frank De Boon, Arnold De Boon, John Denengelsen and Geralyn Hoffman.

Lone Pine Publishing would like to thank Maris Vecmanis of Totem Outdoor Outfitters for his close reading of the manuscript and his valuable suggestions. Lone Pine also acknowledges the efforts of the Waterton Lakes Natural History Association, and the input of Parks Canada. As well, the continuing support of Alberta Culture and The Alberta Foundation for the Literary Arts is gratefully acknowledged.

PHOTO CREDITS

The authors are especially grateful to those who contributed the use of their photographs to this publication. Special gratitude is extended to Wayne Roberts, Sandra Gibbon, Leon Carl, David Donald, Frank De Boon, John Denengelsen, Simon Lunn and Dave Romanuck.

Additional photo contributors include Bob Purdy, Mel Kozun, Rich Rothwell, Elaine Butler, Arnold De Boon, Stan Clements, Ken Goble, Donovan Saul, John Fraley, Heather Proctor and The Peter Whyte Foundation, Archives of the Canadian Rockies, and Waterton Lakes National Park.

Fish anatomy diagram from *A Practical Guide to the Anatomy and Physiology of Pacific Salmon* by L.S. Smith and G.R. Bell (Fisheries and Marine Service, Miscellaneous Special Publication 27, Ottawa, 1975) is used by permission.

Special thanks to Luellen Bevan "Martin" for the use of her family photos.

Contents

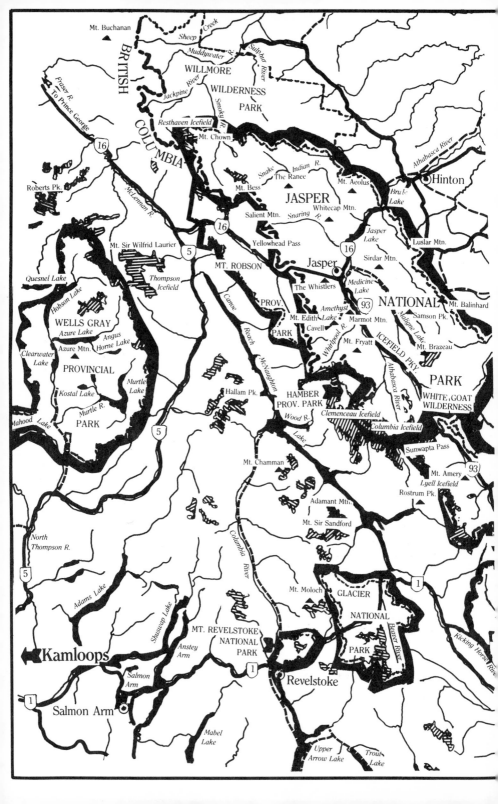

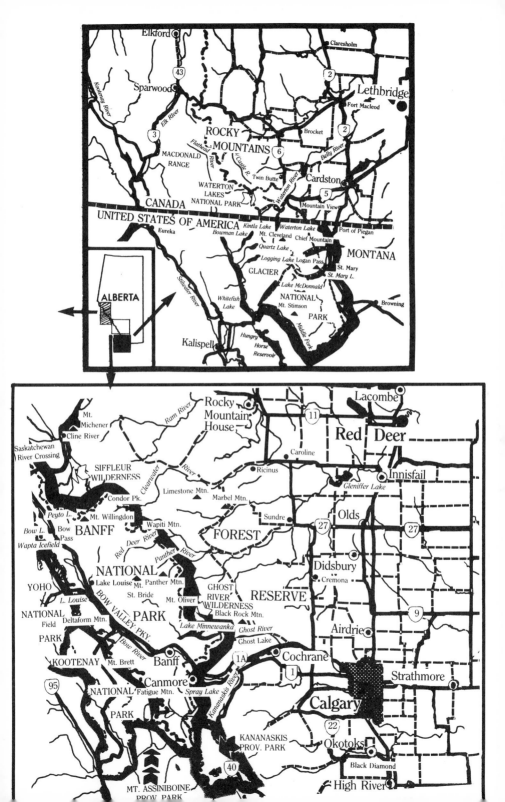

INTRODUCTION

This book is designed for anglers, fishwatchers, amateur naturalists, or anyone else who enjoys the magic of lakes, streams and rivers and the fish that occupy them. The book is intended to meet a long-requested need for a condensed, yet comprehensive, identification guide to all the sport fish an angler might encounter while fishing in the Rocky Mountains. It will particularly serve those people fishing the National Parks of Waterton Lakes, Banff, Jasper, Yoho, Kootenay and Glacier National Park, Montana and the wilderness areas which adjoin them. This book is not intended to be a lake-by-lake or stream-by-stream analysis. Such information and the current fishing conditions specific to each location may vary widely from week to week or year to year. Details of this nature are best obtained from a local specialty angling store. Information on guides, boat rentals and local fly patterns are also likely to be available. Fishing is spoken at these places and good sound advice is freely offered to those who merely ask.

At many local sport shops and stores you can also purchase the

Sandra Gibbon

The headwaters of the Clearwater River in Banff National Park. Such waters are important rearing locations for young bull trout and mountain whitefish.

necessary national parks, provincial or state fishing licenses. Anyone fishing in a national park will need to purchase the national parks fishing licence. It is the only licence necessary while in Canada's national parks. In either Alberta or British Columbia you will need to purchase the appropriate provincial fishing licences. In Glacier National Park, Montana, no state licence is required, but a park fishing permit is required. The permit is free.

Make yourself familiar with the fishing seasons, possession and daily catch limits for the area you plan to fish. Government officers regularly patrol fishing waters. A visit by the local ranger should add rather than detract from the fishing trip.

This book attempts to provide some insight into the specific nature of the varied aquatic environments of the mountain parks. It describes from an angler's perspective how these environments affect the fish which occupy mountain habitats. The range of photographs also provides visual clarification for those seeking to identify habitats utilized by sport fish. The book also examines some practical and ethical considerations for anglers who pursue trout and other sport fish which live in the parks.

The individual descriptions cover the eighteen important and less important species of fish anglers are likely to encounter. References are made where appropriate to additional species or to distinctive genetic varieties. Identification information contains a minimum of technical jargon. It is complemented by supportive color and black-and-white photographs. Visual material is selected to demonstrate the most recognizable characteristics for that species, or a relevant facet of their life history. With each species, information is provided on the fish's habits, food and habitat preferences, spawning behavior and distribution. Further angling information beyond these categories is also included for each species.

The book also tries to make the point that angling for wild-spawned fish in the environment of a national park is a privilege. It is an opportunity very different from fishing in a hatchery-stocked reservoir. There is far more to this opportunity than catching fish. Angling is only one part of a mountain fishing experience. The fish themselves are so fascinating that the opportunity to observe and understand more about them may be ample reward for a visiting angler. It is our hope that this book will contribute to that fascination and provide a more meaningful and fulfilling interaction with the naturally occurring sport fish of the Canadian and Montana Rockies.

Government Sources

The following government sources may be contacted for information:

●Banff National Park
c/o Superintendent
Box 900
Banff, Alberta
T0L 0C0

●Information Center
224 Banff Avenue
Phone: 403-762-4256

●Jasper National Park
c/o Superintendent
Box 10
Jasper, Alberta
T0E 1E0

Information Center
500 Connaught Street
Phone: 403-857-6176

●Kootenay National Park
c/o Superintendent
Box 220
Radium Hot Springs, B.C.
V0A 1M0

Visitor Information Center
(West Gate at Radium Hot Springs)
Phone: 604-347-9615

●Waterton Lakes National Park
c/o Superintendent
Waterton Park, Alberta
T0K 2M0

Information Center
Phone: 403-859-2445

●Yoho National Park
c/o Superintendent
Box 99
Field, B.C.
V0A 1G0

West Information Center
(32 km west of Field on Trans-Canada Hwy.)
Phone: 604-343-6484

East Information Center
(3 km east of Field on Trans-Canada Hwy.)
Phone: 604-343-6324

●Glacier National Park (U.S.A.)
c/o Superintendent
West Glacier
Montana 59936

Apgar Visitor Center
(West side of Apgar)
Phone: 406-888-5441

St. Mary's Visitor Center
(East Side)
Phone: 406-732-4424

●Glacier National Park
or
Mt. Revelstoke National Park
P.O. Box 350
Revelstoke, B.C.
V0E 2S0

●Willmore Wilderness Area
Energy and Natural Resources
Information Center
9920 - 108 Street
Edmonton, Alberta
T5K 2M4
403-427-3590

●Mt. Robson Provincial Park
District Superintendent
Box 579
Valemont, B.C.
V0E 2Z0
604-566-4325

●William A. Switzer Provincial Park
Box 1038
Hinton, Alberta
T0E 1B0
403-865-7504

●Beauvais Lake Provincial Park
P.O. Box 1810
Pincher Creek, Alberta
T0K 1W0
403-627-2021

●Bow Valley Provincial Park
Information Center
Box 280
Exshaw, Alberta
T0L 2C0
403-673-3663

●Kananaskis Country
412, 1011 Glenmore Trail S.W.
Calgary, Alberta
T2V 4R6
403-297-3362

●Alberta Fish and Wildlife
(Fisheries Services Branch)
5th Floor
9920 - 108 Street
Edmonton, Alberta
T5K 2M4
403-427-6730

●Fish and Wildlife Branch (B.C.)
Kootenay Regional Headquarters
320 Ward Street
Nelson, B.C.
V1L 1S6
604-352-2211

●Fish and Wildlife Branch (B.C.)
Omineca—Peace Regional Headquarters
1777 - 3rd Avenue
Prince George, B.C.
V2L 3G7
604-562-8131 (Loc. 360)

FISHING IN A NATIONAL PARK

Knowing the Environment

For many park anglers, trout simply live in the environments they themselves most enjoy visiting. There is a magic that results from being beside water. The natural integrity of the surrounding environment, whether subtle or majestic, has often been best preserved under park stewardship. In general the diverse landscapes of our national parks have also been destined to satisfy the many appetites of a highly

David Donald

Lake O'Hara in Yoho National Park has a natural spawning population of cutthroat trout in a remarkably scenic setting. The turquoise blue colouring is due to light scattered by the suspended glacial silt in the water. Such glacial silt reduces productivity but does not eliminate it.

demanding society.

In the national parks, an angler can still find solitude, and fish all day without meeting another angler. There are, however, others fishing. It may be the loon, the grebe, the merganser, the great blue heron silently waiting, or even the active osprey with an eye mask to reduce glare and a foot surface rough with spicules—a sandpaper grip for slippery trout.

Most of the daily events and dramas occurring along a trout stream are subtle. An angler must tune in to the surroundings to become aware of them. It may be the quiet ripple of a tiny water shrew foraging underwater for a longnose dace, or the drama of an emerging mayfly as it struggles to unfold its wings in the surface tension of a protected eddy. When you miss seeing a trout strike at your fly because your eyes are diverted from its drift path, following instead the streamside foraging of a Wilson's warbler or cedar waxwing, then you have arrived at the larger perspective. You are enjoying the fullest form of the angling experience.

Roderick Haig-Brown in his *Fisherman's Spring* wrote of such matters in this way:

> ... *it seems clear that a man is missing something if he does not know the drumming of a ruffed grouse from the hoot of a blue grouse, if he cannot tell an eagle from an osprey or a merganser from a goldeneye. Birds share a fisherman's world and are part of his scene.*

There are, of course, more pragmatic reasons for anglers to pay close attention to birds. Birds that capture flying insects on the wing are wonderful indicators that an insect hatch is underway. They frenzy in the air at these opportunities in the manner that trout frenzy below the water's surface. The feeding flights of Eastern kingbirds, other flycatchers like the olive-sided, willow, alder, and ruby-crowned kinglets, and Wilson's and Audubon's warblers have all proven to be important indicators of highly rewarding hatches.

Field of Vision of the Trout (p. 19): Light from the surface of a body of water is refracted into the eyes of the trout as two cones, each with an arc of about 97°. Underwater, the trout's vision extends in all directions, except for a 30°-wide swath that stretches below and behind him and is his blind spot.

Angling Etiquette

Extending this general awareness to the presence of other anglers is an additional consideration. It assures a satisfying experience for all concerned. There are unspoken codes of preferred angling behavior, and when the codes are violated, the pleasure is likely to be diminished.

Elbow room is one of the basic principles of stream manners. Any pool or reasonably definable reach of water belongs to the first person fishing it. As well, whether he or she is moving upstream or down, it is inconsiderate to start fishing ahead of this person. The distance between you and other fishermen varies with the size of the water and how well you know them. One hundred feet is perhaps a minimal buffer zone.

Walking thoughtlessly along a bank in plain view of a fisherman's trout is an obvious offence. Give a wide berth. Mountain trout are always more wary than expected. When fishing the same stretch of river as another fisherman, carefully leave the river and walk around when passing, taking care not to wade noisily nor pass too close.

Avoid such practices as: standing beside a pool being fished by another angler (especially if in a white shirt or other reflective clothing);

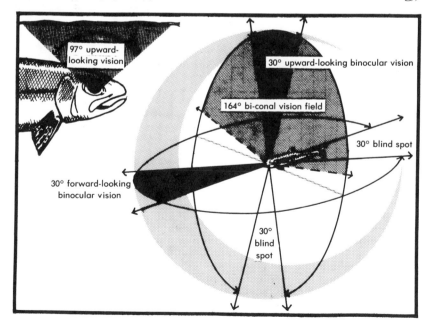

John Denengelsen

Common Loon

Simon Lunn

Bald Eagle

Frank de Boon

Red-necked Grebe

James Butler

Northern Water Shrew

leaning over a bridge railing above an angler working a pool; walking past another fisherman in full silhouette against the sky, even some distance from the water.

It would be inconsiderate to watch at close distances a person fishing a pool without asking if it disturbs them, let alone to permit your family to conduct a free-for-all along the bank. Be careful about getting into a pool that is already being fished, even on the most crowded streams, without first asking the other fishermen's permission.

When invited to fish with someone, the invitation is limited to you alone, and you should not add anyone else to the party without permission.

Brief conversation with a fellow fly-fisherman is an obvious courtesy, but extended dialogue without invitation is another matter. Shattering the silence enjoyed by an angler or disturbing their concentration by loudly accosting the angler to enquire about what they are catching or what fly they are using, will always be bad manners so long as there are quiet streams.

One unspoken rule applies absolutely when being taken to fish a new lake or reach of river by a friend. To show that secret place to another angler is a betrayal of the sacred trust between fishing comrades.

Fishwatching

There are many park visitors for whom watching fish can just as much fun as catching them. A hook and line are not essential to find those shady secret pools or bright fast water, nor to enjoy an encounter with the fish that dwell there. All it takes is a quick eye, a healthy

Wayne Roberts

Bull trout frequently rest on the bottom in this fashion, more so than other species. Their broad flat head may even assist them in allowing the current to press them against the bottom. This young male was about 17" (43 cm) in length.

curiosity and a little time. The use of sunglasses with polarizing lenses will greatly aid in observing fish. After all, it is the water and the overall environment that are magical; the fish simply provide a focus for the exercise.

Thousands of visitors travel annually to watch the sockeye spawn in the Adams River of British Columbia or the kokanee at McDonald Creek in Glacier National Park, Montana. Hundreds of hikers seek out the inlets and outlets of alpine lakes to watch the cutthroat spawn. Park visitors to Elk Island National Park can be observed lying on the boardwalk planking for hours, watching the actions of stickleback. Even anglers with rod and reel on their lap can be observed sitting motionless, with active feeding trout on all sides, far more absorbed in watching the trout feed than in catching them. Fishwatching is more popular than most suspect and it qualifies as a legitimate outdoor recreation activity.

Some fishwatchers are more active in their pursuit, where the ultimate challenge is to be stealthy enough to touch a fish in the wild. Patience and skill are needed to slowly approach and then lightly stroke the fish along its side—a thrill few fishermen have experienced.

Catch-and-Release

The modern angler's fish stories may not be about the number of fish kept or the one that got away, but about the number of fish that were released for another day. His creel may contain an occasional fish, if there is a desire to eat fresh fish, or it may be a fish that has been injured through an unfortunate hooking and cannot be released successfully. But many skilled fishermen love their sport far too much to spoil it with wanton killing. Catching and releasing trout is a kind of ritual ceremony that satisfies both our achievement motives, and our mixture of reverence and respect for the beauty and courage of the trout.

Catch-and-release also makes good sense for the immediate area. Many fishermen travel hundreds of miles to fish a stream or lake amidst the scenic splendor of the mountain parks, paying astonishing amounts of money in terms of each pound of fish caught. Catch-and-release helps to ensure that fish populations remain high enough to make return trips worthwhile.

Jim Butler

Catch-and-release regulations are an excellent way to ensure angling opportunities for the growing numbers of visitors to our National Parks. The continued support of anglers toward such expanded regulations is necessary if future generations are to experience the magic of encountering a wild trout in the splendor of our mountain parks.

Angling as a preferred recreational activity does not require manipulation of the natural scenery. Other resource pressures, real and potential, seem far more likely to degrade these mountain environments than angling ever will. In summary, streams, lakes and trout need as many friends as they can get. The integrity of their environment and all those organisms which share these special places depend upon friends to survive.

Trout Pedigree

An additional matter that can contribute to a quality angling experience is the growing preference to seek and value trout more for their genetic heritage and pedigrees than for their size. Remote native genetic stocks unaffected by hatchery introductions are increasingly valued by some anglers, even though the fish are often stunted in size because they occur in small headwater tributaries.

Sport fishing is more than just catching fish. It is a special time to escape the pressures of everyday life, experience a sense of adventure and just take the opportunity to appreciate the splendors of nature in a national park. In many cases fishing provides a focus for a relaxed social outing. The fisherman in this instance is not just an individual but a member of a group, and sharing the experience is an important dimension of it.

Rich Rothwell

The diminutive Athabasca rainbow trout is a distinctive genetic stock which occurs only in the headwaters of the Athabasca River watershed in and near Jasper National Park. This adult female is full size.

FISH MANAGEMENT
IN MOUNTAIN PARKS

A century ago, Canada began a system of national parks. During the initial years, there was an emphasis on the exploitation of these unique areas. This emphasis on exploitation extended to the fish populations. Indeed, the lure for many early visitors was due, in part, to the fishing opportunities.

Early park visitors and residents like Walter Wilcox told of wonderful fishing trips in the national parks. In 1906, Julia Henshaw wrote an article titled, "A Fisherwoman in the Rockies." She described how "in an hour, thirteen trout varying from one-half to two lbs. would be in my creel." Indeed, the attitude by the visitors and others was that the fish resources were inexhaustible.

Archives of Canadian Rockies, Peter Whyte Foundation

Early fishing success in Banff.

As early as 1900 commercial outfitters were advertising fishing expeditions, and by 1913 the park lodges were registering more than 60,000 guests annually. Due to increased fishing pressures, the inevitable decline in these natural stocks occurred. As a response, fishing regulations in the form of limits, seasons and closures were instituted in an effort to protect the remaining stocks. From 1913 to 1970, extensive rearing and stocking programs were in operation to increase the recreational fishing potential for all the mountain parks. There was very little early concern given to the maintenance or protection of naturally occurring fish stocks. The primary concern was to produce fish for the creel, i.e., "put and take."

Practically every body of water was affected by these stocking programs. In several cases, exotic fish such as Quebec red trout and Atlantic salmon were brought into the mountain parks.

Because of abundant food supplies, formerly barren lakes produced large trout very quickly after receiving stocked fish. After a period of time, the lake ecosystems eventually reached an equilibrium. In many of these lakes, the stocked fish soon disappeared because of inadequate oxygen levels during the winter or lack of adequate spawning areas. In some lakes, a few of the larger fish completely monopolized the food supply, growing to extreme sizes.

In waters where exotic species were introduced, competing with native species for food and spawning areas, the exotic species would dominate, causing the natives to decline or disappear altogether. Exotic species often hybridized with native stocks. The sport fish became the most manipulated animals in the national parks.

Beginning in 1960, there were significant changes in policy regarding fish. Many more ecological considerations emerged concerning the fish stocking/hatchery programs. In 1957, both the Banff and Waterton Lakes hatcheries were closed down, although the Jasper hatchery was expanded. In 1972, as a result of a viral infection and apparent lack of success in stocking high mountain lakes, the Jasper hatchery was closed. Even though the park-operated hatcheries were closed down, stocking of some fish continued.

In 1979, with the development of the current Parks Canada Policy, all stocking programs were restricted, although limited stocking still takes place. Under this new policy, naturally regenerating populations of native species are favoured. Restrictions and regulations are also more effectively applied to protect the ecosystem and maintain fish populations. Non-native species of fish are not to be introduced into a park, and where they already exist, Parks Canada will try to remove them.

Luellen Bevan

*The early fish hatchery in Banff. The residence is in the
background, with a display pond containing large specimens of
trout in the foreground. Other display ponds with smaller fish are
to the right.*

In Alberta, new government regulations limit the daily catch in high
mountain lakes to two trout. The same limit (daily catch of two) has
been applied to golden and bull trout caught in any waters.

National parks in the United States and in adjacent provinces in
Canada have established stream zoning, fly-fishing-only designations and
catch-and-release regulations, with widespread success. While
conscientious anglers employ such practices as catch-and-release as if
mandatory, improved regulations in concert with expanded research are
necessary to usher in a modern era of fisheries management.

FISHING ENVIRONMENTS OF THE MOUNTAIN PARKS

Streams and Rivers

Angling in moving waters

Every angler will see something slightly different as he or she views the moving waters. It is no accident that less than five per cent of all anglers catch more than 50 per cent of the fish taken. The successful angler will get inside the trout's scales and begin to think like a trout. It is important to consider the need for shelter, resting areas and, of course, feeding sites. Where the water in the stream moves the fastest, such as in the center near the surface, the energy expenditure required by a fish to stay there and feed is often too high in comparison to the

Mel Kozun

Elaine Butler

Swift mountain waters pose a special challenge to the angler. In such places as this, well-weighted lures or flies may be productive when worked in the eddies, where quiet water meets swift water.

Always look over the stream carefully before you approach and begin to cast. Approach quietly and lightly, avoiding quick movement. Clothing should be neutral in color and should blend with your surroundings.

energy intake from the food obtained. The balance is often a narrow one. Areas of lower water velocities, where the energy demands are minimized, are essential for energy-efficient feeding sites. They occur, for instance, behind rocks or stumps, in the eddy of a stream curvature or in depressions on the bottom of the stream bed.

Reading a stream or river is seeing and understanding the significance of holes, rapids, riffles, boulders, gravel bars, snags and overhanging vegetation. All of these features act upon and affect how a particular individual or species of fish goes about making a living in that environment. Probably the most important consideration for the sport angler is the nature of the food being consumed. Larvae, adult insects, zooplankton, forage-fish species and other nutrients available to fish will differ dramatically according to the microclimatic differences created by channel shapes, obstructions, substrate (or bottom) differences and water depths. A stream or river will contain shallow edges, quiet runs and pools, fast water, eddies and backwaters. Each is a distinctive environment and requires its own individualized angling approach.

Jim Butler

Mountain streams like the headwaters of the Astoria in Jasper National Park are relatively nutrient rich, and prove to be important rearing areas for young fish. The algae and mosses harbor many invertebrates, and the rocks provide good holding water.

29

Trout lying in a depression — side view

Trout lying in a depression — top view

Rainbow Trout holding around a boulder — side view

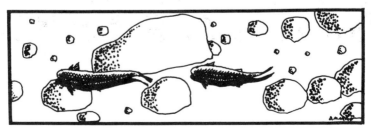

Rainbow Trout holding around a boulder — top view

Shallows and quiet runs

The shallow edges for the most part are nurseries for aquatic insects and small fish, especially if there is overhanging vegetation, aquatic or emergent vegetation or clean gravel with silt-free spaces. Larger fish will often feed alongside or just downstream of these areas.

Quiet runs are most common following deep, fast-water areas. These quiet areas are favorite feeding sites for fish in the evening and early mornings, both on the surface and bottom. Many bottom-dwelling larvae of insects such as mayflies, caddisflies and stoneflies can be found here, especially if there is a gravel bottom. Stream invertebrates (insects, larvae, etc.) are rarely free-swimming but graze and move slowly about the gravel and rocks, eating algae or smaller prey. Some, like certain caddisfly larvae or mayfly nymphs, simply attach themselves and stay put, straining and feeding on passing foods. Often fish will forage in these quiet gravelled areas.

Fish are attracted to these quiet areas when the aquatic insects change into their adult flying forms, especially mayflies and caddisflies. These adult hatches can be quite dramatic both in terms of insect numbers and the frenzied fish feeding. Such a hatch, common in early evening following a day of sunshine, is what anglers most hope for. Watch for these hatches and use the appropriate fly to mimic the aquatic insects. The rising fish can be highly selective with so many "naturals" on the water, and your dry fly must come close to "matching the hatch" in the size, color and general outline of the hatching insect. As well, the imitation must be floated naturally with the current. Casting upstream and across will normally produce the most realistic drift. Record in your mind the exact locations of rising fish and systematically cast to individuals each in succession. With each catch, be conscious of minimizing disturbance to the next fish in the sequence.

Maligne River   Sandra Gibbon   *Martin Creek*   David Donald

Mountain streams may be clear like the Maligne River or glacially silted, such as Martin Creek. Glacial-fed, silted streams are generally less productive, although bull trout and mountain whitefish persist in these habitats. Clear streams are generally warmer, and a surprising number of small invertebrates are present despite the appearance of sterility. Areas fed by ground water are considerably warmer than snow-fed areas. This contributes to increased productivity.

Riffles and fast water

Riffles are often used as forage areas and tend to be very productive because of the excellent light penetration and clean, well-aerated gravels which are valuable habitats for many fish-food invertebrates. Many aquatic insects inhabit the rocky subsurfaces. As these aquatic insects move about foraging, they are exposed or washed free, making them available to the trout. Flies or lures that mimic these aquatic insects or the smaller fish found in these areas are often productive. Areas where riffles meet pools are always important angling locations, with the fish lying at the junction of these two distinctive environments. Cast well up into the riffle and allow your fly or bait to drift into and through the pool.

In moving waters, most fish play a waiting game by selecting an energy-efficient hold within the visible proximity of free-floating foods. Fish may forage through areas of high energy demand, withstanding current resistance for short periods, but the rewards must be worth it.

Frank de Boon

Fishing the tail water of a pool in a large mountain stream. Such habitats are ideal for bull trout and mountain whitefish. Casting up and across the current with a nymph, streamer or bucktail could be productive here.

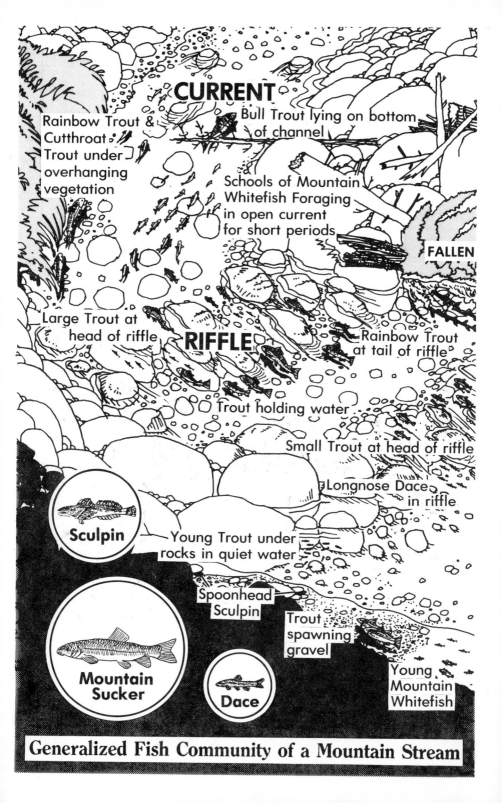

Generalized Fish Community of a Mountain Stream

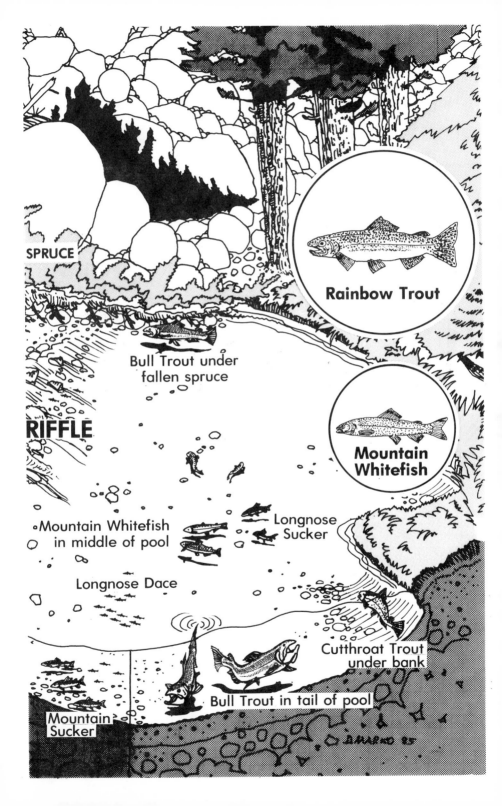

SPRUCE

Rainbow Trout

Bull Trout under
fallen spruce

RIFFLE

Mountain
Whitefish

Mountain Whitefish
in middle of pool

Longnose
Sucker

Longnose Dace

Cutthroat Trout
under bank

Mountain
Sucker

Bull Trout in tail of pool

Mountain Lakes

Amethyst Lake in the Tonquin Valley of Jasper National Park is a typical oligotrophic lake (i.e. low in nutrients and high in oxygen). Despite its reputation for excellent rainbow and brook trout fishing, production is only half that for lakes in the Athabasca Valley, near Jasper townsite.

Still-water angling

High alpine lakes are typically sites of low nutrient production, and fish are often stunted in such areas. The growing season of maximum plant and insect productivity is very short, forcing the fish to feed on a large number of small organisms which is energy expensive. Stunted fish populations are characteristic of high mountain lakes. This is especially noticeable for brook, rainbow and lake trout. In such unproductive lakes, food organisms are scarce and the fish numbers are high. Also, cold water for cold-blooded animals will slow the rate at which they can digest and assimilate food. In cold water trout are efficient at turning food to trout flesh but it takes a long time.

Fish in these cold lakes, in addition to their stunting, can reach extreme old age. The stunted lake trout shown will live to 30-40 years. Longnose suckers commonly live to over 20 years of age. One stunted longnose sucker from Kootenay National Park proved to be at least 31 years of age when caught. Cold water on a cold-blooded fish greatly slows the metabolism, especially when that fish's environment does not require the energy expenditure of fighting currents. The pace is slow and easy in alpine lakes. A brook trout in the warm temperature of a prairie pond will metabolically burn itself out in five years. That same brook trout in a cold mountain lake can reach the incredible old age of 25.

High mountain lakes are also distinctive for their sharply limited diversity of fish species. Visitors not accustomed to fishing in mountain or arctic environments must adjust quickly to the fact that these lakes rarely contain more than two species, and most often just one.

Anglers venturing into the mountains in anticipation of a scenic wilderness fishing excursion are often surprised to discover that many mountain lakes do not become ice-free until July or even August. At some lakes, in certain years the ice may never leave. It pays to inquire about lake conditions before embarking on a backcountry trip.

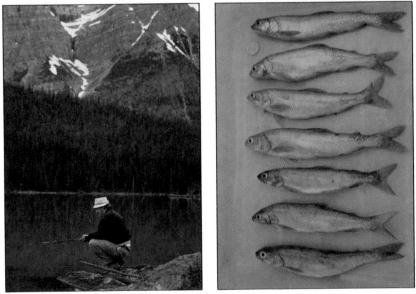

David Donald   Elaine Butler

High lakes have low nutrient availability, cold temperatures and short seasons of maximum productivity. In addition, being forced to feed on a large number of small organisms is energy expensive for fish. Stunted populations are the result. These are full size lake trout from Sassenach Lake in Jasper National Park. All are at least twenty years old.

Profile of a Mountain Lake

Depth and temperature in alpine and montane lakes

In alpine, subalpine, and montane lakes of the mountain parks the general productivity of fish for angling depends upon the water depth. Extensive areas of deep water greatly inhibit a lake's angling potential. Lakes can be very shallow, such as Beaver Lake in Jasper National Park with the deepest spot only about six feet (2 meters); or lakes can be considerably deeper, such as Maligne Lake, also in Jasper with a depth of 300 feet (92 meters). A depth of 200 feet (60 meters) is considered deep for lakes in the mountain national parks. Only six lakes reach depths in excess of this: Marvel, Louise and Minnewanka in Banff National Park; Maligne of Jasper; McArthur of Yoho National Park; and Upper Waterton Lake, the deepest of the system, having a maximum depth of 487 feet (148 meters).

Warm water contributes to higher productivity, and shallow lakes, usually of seepage origin such as Beaver Lake, may attain surface temperatures of 77°F (25°C) in late summer. Cold, deep glacier-fed lakes, such as Maligne, rarely exceed surface temperatures of 45°F (13°C).

The best places for fishing can almost always be reached from the shore. In large, deep lakes both fish and lake-dwelling aquatic insects associate almost exclusively with the shoreline and the bottom of a lake near the shore (littoral zone). Here occurs the greatest variety of potential food organisms, and it is also the preferred feeding location for organisms which dwell on the lake bottoms. The circumstances of a prairie lake are virtually the reverse—a boat is needed for fishing to get into the lake beyond the littoral zone. In deep lakes of the mountain parks, boats usually serve only for ease of casting and access, except perhaps when trolling for lake trout, or lake whitefish.

Lake food sources for trout

Knowing what a trout eats makes angling easier. Extensive lake studies of brook and rainbow trout food preferences suggest that about 90 per cent of the diet is made up from equal proportions of caddisflies (*Trichoptera*), midges (*Chironomidae*), and amphipods or scuds (*Amphipoda*).

The presence of amphipods, specifically the tiny olive scud, *Hyalella azteca*, and the olive freshwater scud, *Gammarus lacustris*, in a lake makes a remarkable difference in the size of the trout in such lakes. Large trout in our mountain lakes are invariably amphipod feeders. Stunted, slow-growing trout populations are often attributed to an absence of amphipods. Upper Jade Lake in Mt. Revelstoke National Park is one such amphipod-free lake, where rainbow trout 10 to 12 years old weigh less than 10 oz. (0.3 kg). The stunted rainbow from Lower Jade Lake in the photo on page 44 was four years old and weighed only 2.8 oz. (0.08 kg). The giant rainbow trout pictured on page 44 from the first of the Five Lakes in Jasper National Park is the product of a lake with an amphipod density of 1,000 to 2,000 per square yard. This fish is less than ten years old, 32 in. (81.9 cm) in length, and weighed 21.3 lbs. (9.76 kg). It pays, therefore, to be able to recognize the presence of important foods when choosing where to spend your time angling.

The recognition of aquatic organisms can also be helpful in other ways. The fairy or freshwater shrimp (the crustacean *Branchinecta*) is such a vulnerable organism that it is consumed completely whenever

Two most common amphipods, or scuds, of lake environments: small Hyallela *and large* Gammarus. *When they occur in a lake, they comprise 80% of a fish's diet.*

Stonefly larvae, Plecoptera, *are an important food in streams but not lakes. Also called, in larvae form, "hellgrammites", nymphs, naiads. Adult: salmonflies.*

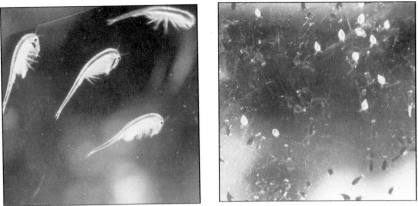

David Donald

David Donald

Fairy or fresh water shrimp (the crustacean Branchinecta*) are virtually consumed completely whenever trout are introduced into their environment. When you see one, the lake is probably fishless.*

Two important members of the zooplankton community are Daphnia (white), also called water flea, whose hatchings peak in June; and fish lice, Diaptomus (red), a valuable trout food source through September and October.

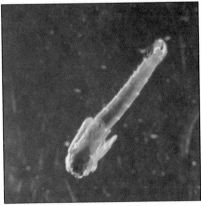

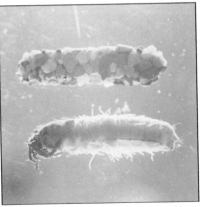

David Donald

David Donald

Midges, Chironomus, *are an extremely important food for trout and whitefish, both in larval form where they resemble a thin segmented worm, and in its developing pupal stage where they occur in high lakes in densities of several thousand per square yard.*

Caddisfly larva, Limephilus, *are common along the shoreline of lakes in the alpine and subalpine. Caddis larva secrete a latex to which stick and harden small particles. Top view is a "rock-roller" studded with pebbles. Bottom shows a "naked" one.*

41

trout are introduced into its environment. When you see it, the lake is fishless. Don't bother wetting a line.

While fish in streams feed almost exclusively by sight, intercepting foods which flow their way in the "drift", fish in lakes are more sensitive to smell. Lake fish locate objects often by swimming or cruising slowly to increase their chances of encountering food. Food is not evenly distributed along the lake margins, but it occurs in patches. Fish cruise the lakes, foraging from patch to patch. "Still-fishing" at known forage areas is often far more productive than casting to spooked trout.

The sight of a large trout cruising the shallows of a lake is guaranteed to pump adrenaline through your system, but trout can be easily spooked in these still waters. Walk softly, and keep a low profile. Always avoid standing upright by the water's edge, and cast with the longest leaders you have, normally 12 feet. Nymphs rather than adult forms are almost always the preferable fly, except when an occasional hatch might stimulate surface feeding. If you stubbornly insist on using dry flies in non-hatch conditions, black ant or adult damselfly imitations will often produce surprising results at any time of the day.

The outlets of alpine and other lakes are important feeding areas for trout because zooplankton and other invertebrates, often scattered at relatively low density throughout the rest of the lake, are funneled at the outflow through a relatively constricted area. Trout strategically located at such a funnel find disproportionately high food volumes (especially copepods such as *Diaptomus*) without expending excessive energy for foraging.

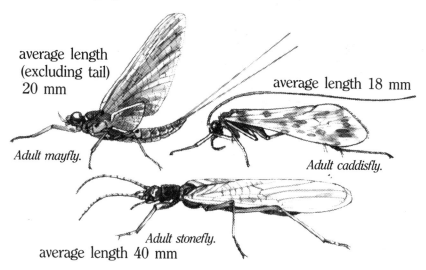

average length (excluding tail) 20 mm

Adult mayfly.

average length 18 mm

Adult caddisfly.

Adult stonefly.

average length 40 mm

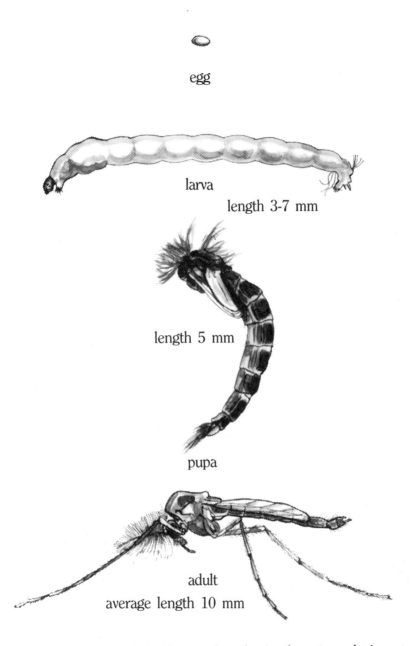

egg

larva

length 3-7 mm

length 5 mm

pupa

adult

average length 10 mm

The stages of insect development, here showing the metamorphosis of a midge. Adults resemble mosquitoes, but without biting parts and with furry antennae.

This giant rainbow trout from the first of the Five Lakes in Jasper National Park is the product of a lake with an amphipod density of 1,000 to 2,000 per square meter. This fish is less than ten years old, 32 inches in length and weighs 21.3 lbs (9.7 kg).

Amphipods are important to fish in mountain lakes. This stunted adult rainbow trout from Lower Jade Lake in Mt. Revelstoke National Park is a product of a lake without amphipods. The fish is four years of age and weighs only 2.8 oz. (0.08 kg).

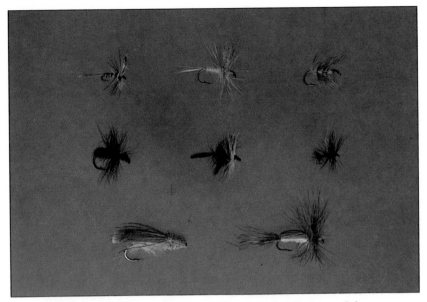

Dry flies commonly used in the mountain parks. Top row (left to right): Mosquito, Light Cahill, Griffith's Gnat. Middle row: Black Ant, Black Bivisible, Black Gnat. Bottom row: Latort Hopper, Yellow-bellied Humpy.

Wet flies commonly used in the mountain parks. Top row (left to right): Pheasant-tailed Nymph, Idaho Nymph, Mosquito. Middle row: Doc Spratley, 52-Buick, Gold-ribbed Hare's Ear. Bottom row: Backswimmer, Muddler Minnow.

Generalized Distribution of Fish through a Mountain Stream

High Gradient
Rapid Flow

Low Water Temperature

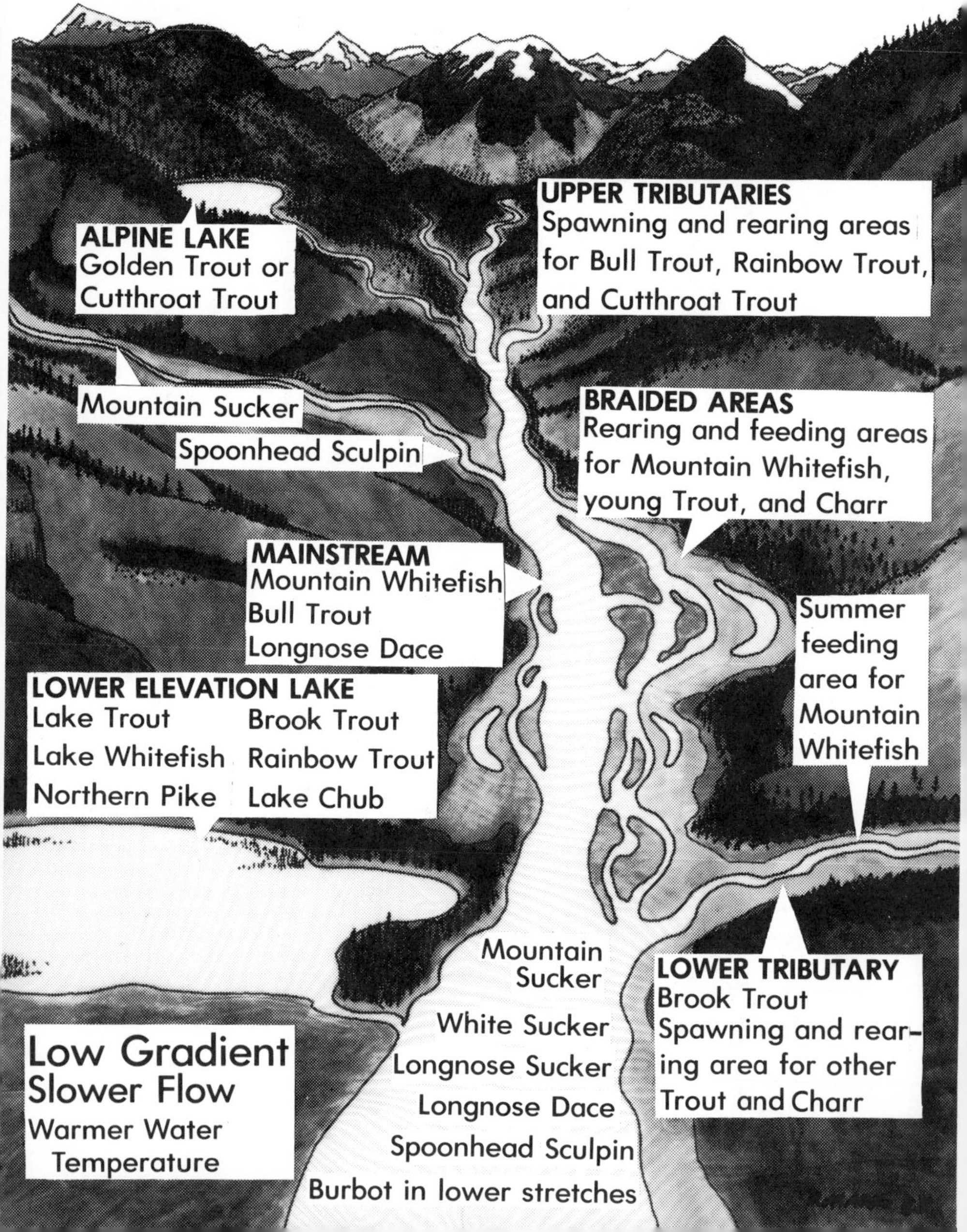

ALPINE LAKE
Golden Trout or
Cutthroat Trout

Mountain Sucker
Spoonhead Sculpin

UPPER TRIBUTARIES
Spawning and rearing areas
for Bull Trout, Rainbow Trout,
and Cutthroat Trout

BRAIDED AREAS
Rearing and feeding areas
for Mountain Whitefish,
young Trout, and Charr

MAINSTREAM
Mountain Whitefish
Bull Trout
Longnose Dace

Summer
feeding
area for
Mountain
Whitefish

LOWER ELEVATION LAKE
Lake Trout   Brook Trout
Lake Whitefish   Rainbow Trout
Northern Pike   Lake Chub

Mountain
Sucker

White Sucker

Longnose Sucker

Longnose Dace

Spoonhead Sculpin

Burbot in lower stretches

LOWER TRIBUTARY
Brook Trout
Spawning and rear-
ing area for other
Trout and Charr

Low Gradient
Slower Flow

Warmer Water
Temperature

IDENTIFYING THE MOUNTAIN FISH

1. Rainbow Trout *Salmo gairdneri*

Family Name: Salmonidae

Other Names: Kamloops trout, Athabasca trout, red-band trout, Steelhead (when they migrate to and from the sea)

Description

The rainbow trout is profusely spotted with distinct black or brown spots, but never with red or white spots. All true trout of genus *Salmo* (rainbow, cutthroat, brown and golden trout) have dark spots while charr (some of which have the common name of trout: brook, bull and lake trout) of the genus *Salvelinus* have light spots. The distinct spots of the rainbow occur on the head, back, throughout the tail and along the sides. Rainbow trout often have a distinctive red streak down the side. The adipose fin (the small fleshy fin on the back, behind the dorsal fin) generally has a black border with pale centre. Rainbow and cutthroat trout (both spring spawners) occasionally hybridize and produce a fish that will have both parental identifying characteristics.

One distinctive genetic stock of rainbow trout is the Athabasca rainbow which occurs in Jasper National Park in the headwaters of the Athabasca River watershed. The Athabasca rainbow is a diminutive stream fish, rarely exceeding 10 in. (25 cm) in length. They do grow well when transplanted to lakes and larger individuals occur in rivers. Note on the photo that they retain distinctive parr marks (dark blotches along their sides) throughout their life. They also generally show a golden tinge on the flap of their operculum (the gill covering). This unique genetic strain of trout is probably the only strain of native rainbow east of the Continental Divide, likely a result of headwater transfers from the upper Fraser River basin. Rainbow were introduced from the west coast into the North Saskatchewan, Bow and Red Deer river drainages in the 1930s.

Leon Carl

Athabasca rainbow trout, like this adult male, retain parr marks throughout their life and often show a golden tinge on the flap of their operculum (gill cover).

Jim Butler

The red stripe is not always present in rainbow trout. They do possess at all times a wide distribution of spots from top to bottom and from the tip of the tail to the tip of the nose.

Comparison of adult male and female rainbow trout from Amethyst Lake, Jasper National Park. Note how the maxilla or the upper jaw extends well beyond the eye of the male. ►

Rainbow Trout

49

Size and Weight

The maximum lengths of the rainbow can be up to 45 in. (114 cm) with weights up to 52.5 lbs. (23.8 kg). In the mountain national parks, there are exceptionally stunted specimens, as well as enormous individuals like the one in the photo from the first of the Valley of Five Lakes in Jasper (the product of abundant amphipods) which weighed 21.5 lbs. (9.76 kg) and was 32.5 in. (81.9 cm) in length. This was the largest rainbow ever found in a Canadian national park. (See photo p. 44)

Distribution

Native to British Columbia, Montana and to Alberta in the Athabasca drainage, the rainbow is now widely scattered throughout the mountain parks. It has been very widely transplanted into these and many other areas of North America and the world.

Life History

Typical of true trout of the genus *Salmo* (the brown trout and Atlantic salmon are exceptions), the rainbow spawn in the springtime. At high altitudes, however, spring may not arrive until July or August. Spawning generally occurs as early as late May to early June in the headwaters of rivers along the east slopes. They prefer gravelly areas in streams, rivers or on lake margins. The female will prepare a redd or nest with her tail where she will deposit 300 to 3,000 eggs, depending on body weight. Since they are laid in the early summer when water temperatures are rising, the eggs develop into fry in as little as four weeks (but usually longer). These small fish feed on smaller adult insects, insect larvae, and crustaceans while foraging in the open, in quiet water near vegetation or near other cover. As the fish grow, they prefer larger insects and fish if available.

Angling

For some rainbow trout populations in the mountain parks where angling pressure is heavy, few fish reach three years of age. In relatively remote unexploited populations, individuals may live to ten years or more. High exploitation serves only to decrease the population numbers as well as the size of the fish caught.

In May and June rainbows are frequently encountered in the spawning streams, or near the shores of mountain lakes immediately following ice breakup. While wet flies are more effective during this time, many park waters are not yet open, so carefully check the regulations. In July and August when the water is warmer, surface feeding is more evident, and dry fly imitations are often more successful.

2. Cutthroat Trout *Salmo clarki*

Family Name: Salmonidae

Other Names: native trout, mountain trout

Description

In the Canadian mountain parks there are at least two subspecies of cutthroat trout, one native and one exotic. All cutthroat trout will have a red or orange slash mark that runs in a groove between the tongue and each lower jaw bone. This red hyoid slash (on the membranes below the gills), from which their name is derived, becomes evident when the fish reaches a length of about three inches, and is used during mouth-gaping territorial displays. The spots on the dorsal (back) and ventral (belly) surfaces vary in size, distribution and frequency, depending on the particular genetic stock. Teeth at the base of the tongue, known as basibranchial teeth, are present in cutthroat but absent in rainbow trout, the fish most likely to be confused with the cutthroat. Cutthroat have relatively small scales when compared to other trout. These scales number usually in excess of 150 along the length of the lateral line. Scales on other trout, including the rainbow, number less than 150. The entire belly may turn red during spawning.

The two forms of cutthroat which occur in the Canadian mountain parks are the west-slope cutthroat, *Salmo clarki lewisi* and the Yellowstone or interior cutthroat, *Salmo clarki bouvieri*. This taxonomy is somewhat different from older reference books, and incorporates recent work of authorities such as Dr. Robert Behnke, who has demonstrated that the interior cutthroat of northwest North America are represented by not one but two distinct forms. The west-slope cutthroat has numerous small spots, especially near the tail on the caudal peduncle (that fleshy area of the tail between the anal fin and tail fin). The spotting is heaviest down the back above the lateral line. The introduced Yellowstone cutthroat has spots which are fewer in number, larger and equally distributed along the sides above and below the lateral line. Many cutthroats will show hybrid characteristics between the two, such as those in Baker Lake of Banff National Park and Sofa Creek of Waterton Lakes National Park.

Size and Weight

Cutthroat trout may reach up to 30 in. (76 cm) in length and weigh up to 22 lbs. (10 kg). Some selected areas in the mountain parks can produce fish in the 11 lbs. (5 kg) range.

David Donald

These spawning Yellowstone cutthroat in Glacier National Park, Montana, are recognized by their fewer and larger spots equally distributed above and below the lateral line. Spring spawning runs in the mountains often coincide with spring floods, a problem which can produce partial year-class failures.

This west-slope cutthroat is distinguished from the Yellowstone subspecies by its small numerous spots distributed mostly above the lateral line down the back. This stout-bodied example is typical in shape for a lake dwelling individual. The red belly occurs only during spawning. The reddish-orange slash under the jaw is also evident. ▶

Frank de Boon

Cutthroat Trout

53

Distribution

The original or native populations of cutthroat trout occurred widely in the southern Canadian mountain parks. Native west-slope cutthroats still occur in at least ten locations; however, most others show the effects of hybridization with other forms of cutthroat or with rainbow trout. Cutthroat are still only found in lakes and streams of the mountains and foothills.

Life History

Spawning occurs in late spring or early summer depending on water temperature and the particular elevation. The female prepares a redd and will spawn from 200-4500 eggs. When the fry hatch in six to seven weeks, their primary food sources are small aquatic insects and other invertebrates. The adults feed on larger invertebrates and small fish. Cutthroat may be subject to partial year-class failures due to spring or summer mountain floods. Severe losses may occur once every ten years or so to stream populations of spring-spawning salmonids.

Angling

Wet and dry flies that resemble natural foods work best on cutthroat trout. Lures and bait can also be used. This trout is not a fussy feeder. The cutthroat is a favorite fly fisherman's fish as it strikes flies and fights well, providing an exciting recreational experience. Studies show that cutthroat respond better to catch-and-release regulations than any other trout species. Their vulnerability to overfishing in streams leaves catch-and-release the recommended approach for this fish, whether or not regulations require their release.

Cutthroat enter tributaries from lakes or larger rivers in May or June, and at such times large numbers may be viewed on gravel bars. These concentrations and the associated spawning activity are well worth hiking in to see in spring, even if the angling season is not yet open. In late summer and fall when the water warms up, cutthroat feed more actively.

3. Brown Trout *Salmo trutta*

Family Name: Salmonidae

Other Names: German brown and Lochleven trout

Description

This golden-brown trout will have rather large dark spots over the back and sides with pale or white halos. There are usually red spots on the sides, but these may be reduced or darkened in fish which occur in large rivers or lakes. No other trout has both red and black spots. (Brook trout usually have red spots along their sides, but being a charr, their spots are light, never dark.) Brown trout have a square tail. The adipose fin is usually without spots as is the tail fin.

Size and Weights

In or near the mountain parks the brown trout may grow as long as 20 in. (50 cm) and weigh up to 4.4 lbs. (2 kg).

Distribution

All brown trout in North America are exotics. In 1883, they were brought to North America from the Black Forest area of Germany. Because the brown can adapt itself to a wide variety of ecological conditions, including the ability to tolerate warmer waters, it has extended its range or been transplanted throughout western North America. It is not common within the mountain parks, but is prevalent in many foothill streams in the immediate vicinity.

Life History

Unlike most other members of the spring-breeding *Salmo* trout, browns spawn in late fall. Because spawning occurs at about the same time as brook trout, sterile hybrids known as "Tiger Trout" occasionally are found. The female brown prepares a redd in gravel areas in streams or rivers. She will deposit 200 to 3,000 eggs, depending on body size. Because the eggs are deposited in the fall, hatching will not occur for several months. The brown prefer various local aquatic insects, both in

This large brown trout with streamer fly is waiting to be released.

Brown trout are often golden in color. This large adult shows the bright red spots on the lower sides that are typical of browns in clear small streams. No other trout has both red and black spots.

This young brown trout has both numerous and large spots which even persist onto the adipose fin, a rare occurrence for the species. This individual is probably 2-3 years old and will probably spawn at age 4 or older. Brook trout, in contrast, may spawn in half this time.

➤

Brown Trout

Slow, warm small creeks with abundant cover are excellent habitats for brook and brown trout.

the larval and adult forms. Older adult browns will also prey extensively on fish. Brown trout are more closely related to the Atlantic salmon, *Salmo salar*, than to the cutthroat and rainbow trout. Anadromous (sea-running) browns along the Atlantic Coast are very similar in appearance to Atlantic salmon while in the ocean.

Angling

The brown is famed for its wariness, and the challenge of testing angling skill against such a wary fish is what contributes to its popularity among selective anglers. Late evening hours are best, as the very large browns are often nocturnal. The fly must be presented to the fish with care and skill or the brown trout will elude the fisherman. Both wet and dry flies will prove successful, but the presentation of the fly is most important. There is good reason why this is the most challenging and highly regarded trout in North America. Some anglers prefer not to kill browns, under the philosophy that a great sport fish deserves to be caught more than once.

While fewer fish are caught during winter-early spring, their average size is usually larger because the smaller fish are less active in the cold weather.

4. Golden Trout *Salmo aguabonita*

Family Name: Salmonidae

Description

The elusive golden trout, with a general body color of light red or gold, sometimes resembles the cutthroat except that it lacks the red slash along each branch of the lower jaw. The fins may be orange-colored while the pelvic and anal fins occasionally have a distinct white tip offset by a black bar. Parr marks (blotches on the sides) are often present in the adults as well as the juveniles. The distinctive black spots are restricted to the area near the tail. When they occur on the back, spots remain, above the lateral line.

At least one current classification system concludes on the basis of minute structural characteristics that the golden trout should be lumped with other rainbow trout under a common heading of red band trout, and should be expressed taxonomically as *Salmo gairdneri aguabonita*.

Size and Weight

Golden trout tend to be smaller than other trout, with lengths up to 18 in. (45 cm) and weights up to 4.4 lbs. (2 kg). Some Alberta lake-dwelling golden trout are giants as far as golden trout go, with individuals over the 4 lbs. (2 kg) mark.

Distribution

Golden trout introduced into Alberta derive from stocks taken from the upper south fork of the Kern River and its tributaries of California. Because of its unique coloration and ability to live in high alpine lakes it has been transplanted to many areas, including some lakes in and near the mountain parks, mostly near Waterton or Kananaskis. Such lakes include South Fork, Gap, Galatea, and Three Isle. At the elevations where it occurs, cutthroat trout are its only expected associates. However, golden trout are generally stocked in waters containing no other fish.

Life History

Spawning takes place during the summer, often in July, when water temperatures are warming and spring finally reaches the high country. They will utilize either lakes or streams with gravel areas. Both the young and adult forms can subsist on plankton if necessary. They will readily utilize other food sources, such as adult insects, larvae and other fish if available.

David Donald

Fish in high alpine lakes such as this are often small due to the low productivity of these environments. Being forced to feed on a large number of small organisms is also energy expensive. Golden or cutthroat trout are typical inhabitants of such places.

Golden trout grow large in Alberta lakes, often exceeding 4 lbs. (1.8 kg.) This male shows the typical sparse spotting with the spots concentrated near the tail. The parr marks, often retained in adults of this species, disappear when the fish is introduced into lakes and large rivers.

➤

Golden Trout

Angling

In general, the angling techniques that work on other trout should prove successful. Catch-and-release methods are preferable to preserve such a distinctive mountain trout. High alpine environments can be relatively nutrient scarce, and the nutrients caught up in an adult golden trout are the product of slow food-chain accumulation. The extraction of a fish prohibits the recycling of these nutrients back into the lake environment. Fish in these rather unproductive alpine lakes are always vulnerable to excessive harvesting as the popularity of backcountry areas increases. Care and skill are necessary to prevent harming the fish. Using flies with barbless hooks is recommended. The golden trout is a worthy fish to meet, and one which requires considerable expenditure of the fisherman's energy. For all Alberta waters, there is a daily catch and possession limit of two golden trout per angler.

Angling for golden trout is always best when the water is warmest, especially during the chironomus (midge) hatches in July-August.

Leon Carl

Releasing a golden trout. Nutrients are relatively scarce in a high alpine environment, and many are accumulated in an adult fish. Extraction of fish from such an environment prohibits the recycling of these nutrients back into the lake environment.

5. Brook Trout *Salvelinus fontinalis*

Family Name: Salmonidae

Other Names: speckled trout, charr, brookie, Nipigon trout

Description

The brook trout is one of the three charr that occur within the mountain parks. The two other charr are the bull and lake trout. All of these charr have light spots rather than dark spots against a darker background, and usually have a leading edge of white followed by black on the pectoral, pelvic and anal fins. There are red spots, some with bluish halos along the lower sides. The dorsal surface or back of the brook trout has numerous light "wormy" lines (vermiculations) rather than spots. The tail is almost square, similar to that of a brown trout. This is a strikingly attractive charr, especially during the spawning season, equalled in beauty only by the more northern relative, the Arctic charr.

Size and Weight

In the mountain parks the brook trout may exhibit extreme stunted growth, so that five-year-olds may weigh only 1.7 oz. (0.05 kg). In other lakes, by contrast, there will be very superior growth and weights in excess of 2.2 lbs. (1 kg) may be attained by age five.

Distribution

All brook trout in the mountain parks are exotics. Originally they occurred around Hudson Bay and eastern North America. They are now widespread in most of the mountain national parks at lower elevations. In some national park waters, such as the Maligne River watershed in Jasper and Cameron Lake in Waterton Lakes, no natural fish populations existed prior to 1928, when brook trout were introduced.

Brook trout have been the fish most frequently planted in the mountain parks since their first introduction in 1908. At least 150 lakes in Banff, Jasper and Waterton Lakes had been stocked up until 1975, when management policy began to favor the maintenance of native species.

Leon Carl

In the brook trout the light spots seem to connect themselves along the back, forming worm-like vermiculations. The white leading edges of the fins are characteristic of all the charr.

Frank de Boon

This flooded shoreline of warm water with abundant vegetation is a good feeding and growing area for young brook trout.

In this comparison of male and female brook trout during spawning, note the long kyped lower jaw in the male. This species is a charr, and the spots are light rather than dark as in the Salmo trout. ➤

Brook Trout

Life History

Brook trout are tolerant of a wide range of habitats. They can be found in streams, rivers, beaver ponds, and some small lakes. Spawning occurs in late fall, usually September to October. The female prepares a redd, usually by digging with her tail, where 300 to 800 eggs are deposited and covered with gravel. In some mountain lakes where no obvious suitable spawning habitats are available, they are known to spawn over small underwater springs. Both the young and adults are versatile feeders, consuming a great variety of aquatic and terrestrial insects in the larval and adult forms. Brook trout sometimes mature remarkably fast, with some spawning individuals as young as two years old.

Normally, few brook trout live beyond five years, with an eight-year-old being ancient. In our mountain parks, as a product of slow growth and cold water temperatures, age is often extended, and 12-year-old brook trout are not uncommon in certain lakes. Some are known to reach 25 years of age.

The four most important factors which affect the growth of brook trout in the mountain parks have been shown to be the water temperature, the level of dissolved minerals in the water, the altitude, and the presence and abundance of scuds as a food source.

Angling

Because they are enthusiastic feeders, brook trout will take both wet and dry flies that resemble naturally occurring insects. They will also take spinners and baits if these are not too large. Brook trout are an excellent sport and eating fish, readily accessible to all anglers at the lower elevations in proximity to developed visitor areas.

Brook trout are one of the best all-temperature trouts, having a wide thermal tolerance. Therefore, they are accessible (regulations permitting) during virtually all seasons. They still feed most actively during periods of warmer temperatures.

6. Bull Trout *Salvelinus confluentus*

Family Name: Salmonidae

Other Names: Dolly Varden (see text below)

Description

The bull trout is a grey-colored fish with pale yellow, orange, or pinkish spots. It has a body rounded in cross-section and during movement up streams and rivers for spawning, the body may be a light brown to yellow color. The spots are small and not as numerous as those found on the lake trout. The pectoral, pelvic and anal fins have a white strip on the leading edges like other charr. The bull trout never acquires the bright breeding reds and blacks of the arctic charr and the spots on the bull trout are always smaller than the pupils of their eyes. Arctic charr spots are normally larger than the pupil. The arctic charr has been unsuccessfully stocked within the mountain parks.

The bull trout and the Dolly Varden: A few words are appropriate concerning the classification of these two fish. Earlier references spoke only of the Dolly Varden, with a range extending from Alberta's east slopes of the Rocky Mountains to the Pacific Ocean. Recent work has demonstrated that those fish east of the Continental Divide and of the inner mountain watersheds are distinctly different from the Dolly Varden of the coastal streams. Thus all of Alberta's "Dolly Varden" are now reclassified and are referred to as bull trout, *Salvelinus confluentus*. The Dolly Varden of coastal British Columbia, Washington and Alaska are classified as *Salvelinus malma*, a separate and distinct species.

There are five main ways (apart from their ranges) to distinguish a bull trout from a Dolly Varden. First, the upper jaw bone (maxilla) is large and curves down behind the mouth on a bull trout as opposed to being straight and slender on the Dolly Varden (see photo comparison). Second, bull trout have an upward projection on the end of the lower jaw, called a symphysial knob. This is lacking in Dollies except in the kyped (or hooked) jaws of spawning males. Third, bull trout have flattened heads in contrast to the roof-like shape on Dolly Vardens. Fourth, the bull trout have their eyes much closer to the top of the head. If you imagine a line or take a measurement from the centre of the eye to the top of the head and then bring that distance forward in the direction of the nostrils, this

In this comparison of the heads of a bull trout and a Dolly Varden, note that the bull trout (bottom) is easily recognized by its large and curving upper jaw bone (maxilla) and the fact that its eyes are closer to the top of the head.

measurement will fall far short of the nostril on a bull trout. But on a Dolly Varden this measurement will extend beyond or fall relatively close to the nostril. The centre of the eye, top of head measurement technique is one of the few reliable methods to separate the juveniles of these two species. Lastly, in many Dolly Varden the pink spots are actually surrounded by a light halo, rarely present on a bull trout.

Size and Weight

Some bull trout can get very large, 52.5 in. (1.28 meters) long, and weigh up to 32 lbs. (12.9 kg). A more typical large bull trout would be 20 in. (50 cm) long, weighing 3.3 lbs. (1.5 kg).

Distribution

The bull trout is native to all the mountain parks, including Kootenay, Yoho and Mt. Robson in British Columbia, and Glacier National Park, Montana. It is most prevalent in the upper reaches of the major rivers.

This mature male bull trout has the bright pink spots typical of most stream-dwelling individuals. The dark pigment in the fins is more pronounced during spawning. Note the well-developed kype on this spawning male. ➤

68

Bull Trout

Life History

Spawning takes place in the fall as is typical of charr, but not as late, usually September. Bull trout move into the springs and tributaries where the female prepares a redd in a gravelly area. The female can be attended by one to four males, with the largest one being dominant. Up to 5,000 eggs may be deposited by the female. Since they are fall spawners, the eggs will not hatch until next spring. The young fish begin feeding on insects and insect larvae, snails, and even other small fish. The adults feed primarily on other fish, especially mountain whitefish, small trout, sculpins and suckers. They prefer lakes, reservoirs, or large rivers most of the year, moving upstream only to spawn.

Angling

Since adult bull trout are primarily fish-eating, spinners, lures or large baits have been the most popular forms of tackle. As the bull trout has declined significantly in numbers in recent years, and is now regarded by many biologists as a threatened species, special measures must be applied to insure the conservation and protection of this native charr. Bull trout can be easily fished out and are absent from much of their former range. Excessive harvesting has resulted from increased angling pressure and a lack of regulatory protection. Many modern anglers have never seen nor caught a bull trout. None were caught in a recent stream sampling survey by biologists in Banff National Park. Concerned anglers now separate this species from the edible trout species of our parks, recognizing that bull trout deserve protection, and must be managed as a catch-and-release species. As with golden trout, there is a daily catch and possession limit of two bull trout for all Alberta waters.

Fly fishing with streamers or Doc Spratley lures to imitate swimming fish is the recommended angling method. Trout do have a remarkable sense of smell, and bull trout seem especially sensitive to the smell of blood. Some anglers take advantage of this by carrying a piece of fresh liver and wiping their fly in the blood.

Bull trout move into headwaters and tributaries in late summer, usually August, and therefore this season offers the greatest availability of large bull trout to the angler. Pre-spawning bull trout caught during this season should, of course, be released. Debarbing the hook will facilitate release. Take pride in catching a bull trout, but take greater pride in knowing that your release of that fish could ensure that future generations of anglers will not just read about it.

7. Lake Trout *Salvelinus namaycush*

Family Name: Salmonidae

Other Names: Mackinaw trout, grey trout, togue

Description

The lake trout lacks the bright coloration of either charr or trout. The body color is grey or silver overlaid with numerous white spots or vermiculations covering the dorsal and lateral surfaces. The caudal (tail) fin is deeply forked. The pectoral, pelvic and anal fins have white leading edges as with most charr.

An experimental hybrid program between the lake trout and brook trout, carried out in Banff as early as 1946, produced a fish known as a splake. This fertile hybrid, once stocked in several lakes, may still reproduce in a few limited locations.

Size and Weight

The lake trout is actively sought because of its size. In larger lakes its length may reach 39 in. (1.0 meter) and its weight up to 44 lbs. (20 kg). Many high mountain lakes contain highly stunted populations rarely exceeding 12 in. (30 cm).

Distribution

Lake trout, while more representative of northern Canadian lakes, do occur in many of the larger lakes in the mountain parks. Its original range included most of the larger lakes of northern North America.

Life History

Spawning takes place in late fall on rocky or gravelly shoals. The female may spawn about 700 to 750 eggs per 1 lb. (.5 kg) of body weight. These fish do not select mates, prepare a redd, or guard the eggs. The eggs simply fall to the bottom and settle into the irregular spaces between rocks where they are fertilized and hatch in about two months. The younger fish feed on small insects and crustaceans. Larger—2 lb. (1 kg)— lake trout begin to feed almost entirely on other fish. The diet may contain almost any fish available.

Jim Butler

In cold, glacier-fed deep lakes such as Maligne Lake in Jasper National Park, the water depth greatly inhibits productivity. Food organisms and fish populations are most prevalent along the shoreline and shallow littoral zones.

Angling

Because lake trout prefer the colder water temperatures, they tend to be restricted to relatively deep, cold lakes. They may be found at all depths but prefer water temperatures of 59°F (15°C) or less. Trolling large metal lures or simulation fish baits in deep water is a popular method of angling. Casting from the shore in early spring or late fall may also prove successful.

Lake trout are cruising predators. Early in the season (June) they are often in the shallows of lake margins and inlets where the water is warmer and food more abundant. Since lake trout feed largely on whitefish, streamers or lures which imitate them may prove successful. Later, in the

Numerous white spots or vermiculations are typical for lake trout. The intensity of color on the fins as shown is more characteristic of the male. ➤

Lake Trout

73

summer, lake trout distribute themselves more widely throughout mountain lakes, but do not necessarily retreat to deep water to avoid the warm water of summer as they would do in warm-water lakes. Cold-water mountain lakes undergo only a narrow range of seasonal temperature variations.

Dave Romanuck

This free-swimming lake trout, photographed at the bottom of Waterton Lake, demonstrates a wide contrast in spotting from the other individual shown. The deeply forked tail fin is characteristic of the species.

8. Kokanee *Oncorhynchus nerka*

Family Name: Salmonidae

Other Names: sockeye, red salmon, landlocked salmon, little red-fish, blue-backs

Description

The kokanee is the permanent freshwater form of the anadromous (able to spend part of life in both salt and freshwater) sockeye salmon of the Pacific coast. In non-spawning condition, the dorsal surface is steel blue to dark blue. There are no distinct markings of any kind anywhere on the body or fins. The ventral surface (belly) is light colored. When spawning season approaches, the body color brightens to shades of red with the head turning dark or shades of olive green. The male develops a hooked jaw or kype. The anal fin will not have less than 13 anal rays, whereas all trout and charr have less than 13 anal rays.

Size and Weight

Small in comparison to other Pacific salmon, the kokanee usually grow to 12 in. (30 cm) and weigh one lb. (.5 kg) or less.

Distribution

The natural sea-run salmon stocks are found in many streams draining into the north Pacific. However, the land-locked kokanee are a prominent part of Waterton-Glacier International Peace Park's attraction, with their fall spawning run into McDonald Creek in the Apgar area of Glacier National Park, Montana.

Life History

Kokanee are fall spawners. From late September to mid-November the Glacier Park kokanee arrive in McDonald Creek, after four growing seasons in Flathead Lake and a subsequent migration through the Flathead River system. Upon arrival in the gravelly spawning areas, the female digs and prepares a redd while the male defends the area from other fish. The 500 to 1,000 eggs are deposited in the redd and then

McDonald Creek (top) is a prime location to view spawning kokanee. Bald eagles from the Northwest Territories, Alberta and Saskatchewan pause here in concentrations during fall migration (bottom) to feed upon them.

The kokanee die after their first and only spawning. The hooked jaw, which is termed a kype, is characteristic of males during this spawning run. ►

Kokanee

fertilized by the male. Like all Pacific salmon, the kokanee die after spawning. The primary food sources while growing are tiny aquatic insects, crustaceans, or zooplankton. The fish do not eat once they have left the lake on their upstream spawning run. The eggs hatch over winter and by summer the fry have completed their 60-mile (100 km) journey downstream to Flathead Lake, where after four seasons the spawning cycle is once again repeated.

Angling

Kokanee salmon can be caught in their lake habitat by using flashers followed by a small pink lure. They may occasionally take wet flies during spawning runs, most likely snapped at out of irritation. Ecologically, this fish provides a great deal of food to other "natural fishermen" in the environment, especially animals like the mink, black bear, grizzly, eagle, osprey and merganser. The annual fall gathering of hundreds of bald eagles to feed on the spawned-out kokanee at McDonald Creek in Glacier National Park is a world-renowned event, attracting thousands of visitors. Kokanee attract far more fish-watchers than anglers to McDonald Creek.

John Fraley

These kokanee have reached their fourth year of growth in Flathead Lake and will soon migrate to spawn some 40 miles (63 km) to McDonald Creek in Glacier National Park, Montana.

9. Arctic Grayling *Thymallus arcticus*

Family Name: Salmonidae

Description

The most distinguishing characteristic of an adult arctic grayling is its long and brilliantly colored dorsal fin. The upper margin of this fin is green in life with pink or red spots, and has grey and rose alternating bands. The long dorsal fin contains at least 16 rays, and the base of the fin is as long as the length of the head in young fish. No other fish having an adipose fin (the fin behind the dorsal and before the tail) has as many rays in the dorsal fin. The back is olive green to black, the sides are silvery to light purple, and the belly is blue-white. The tail, or caudal fin, is prominently forked. There are usually a few black spots on the front half of the body behind the gills. The young have 12 to 16 parr marks along their sides like most salmonids.

Size and Weight

Throughout their range arctic grayling are not large. In Jasper, their size may be up to 14 in. (35 cm), with weights up to 2.2 lbs. (1 kg). Most are considerably smaller.

Distribution

The arctic grayling occur nearly circumpolar and are a common species in most streams and rivers in northern Alberta. They occur naturally in a limited number of locations in Willmore Wilderness and Jasper National Park (such as Moab Lake) but they do not occur south of Jasper. When some anglers in the Banff vicinity speak of grayling, they are referring to the mountain whitefish, *Prosopium williamsoni.*

Life History

Arctic grayling prefer cold, clear streams or lakes. They are also very sensitive to pollution and overfishing. Spawning occurs in shallow streams as soon as the ice melts. The female does not build a redd but deposits the sticky eggs over gravel or coarse sand. About 7,000 eggs per female are deposited (a trout may deposit about 700); they hatch in two to three

Rich Rothwell

The Embarass River, near Robb, Alberta, is a typical stream habitat for arctic grayling.

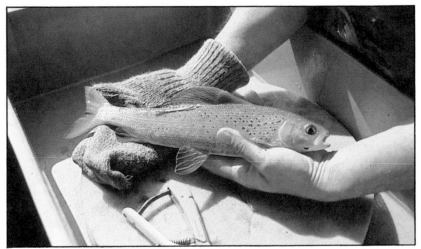

Leon Carl

The grayling is a popular sport fish wherever it occurs. Tagging these fish supplies valuable life history data to biologists assisting in the management and potential introduction of the species.

The large dorsal fin with the white spots in the fin membrane is the most identifiable feature of the arctic grayling. Note the few dark spots on the front part of the body. Also, the arctic grayling is one of the few fish to have orange-colored stripes on the pelvic fins. ►

80

Arctic Grayling

weeks. The young feed on a variety of aquatic insects and insect larvae, both aquatic and terrestrial. Very few fish are included in the diet.

Angling

Because of the arctic grayling's high dependence on insects, fly fishing is the preferred angling method. Use either wet or dry flies that resemble natural foods and present them with caution and care. Dark to black dry flies are a favorite among stream fishermen. These fish prefer open water and are active during the daytime. As grayling are normally easy to catch where they occur, they are vulnerable to overfishing. The grayling of our small streams should invariably be released after being caught.

Grayling ascend tributaries from lakes in the spring but will completely leave these small streams by late summer. They are not 'home-bodies' like trout, which may live their entire life within a small stretch of stream. A location which provides excellent grayling fishing in June or July may be totally devoid of fish in September, although young fish will persist longer in these streams than adult fish.

Leon Carl

In this comparison of male and female arctic grayling, note how the base of the longer dorsal fin of the male (top) is generally longer than the head.

10. Lake Whitefish *Coregonus clupeaformis*

Family Name: Salmonidae

Description

The lake whitefish is a robust silvery fish with a laterally (side-to-side) compressed body. The scales are large with darkened margins. The caudal (or tail) fin is deeply forked. All fins may have dark pointed tips. There are two flaps of skin which divide each of the nostrils, whereas the mountain whitefish has only one flap of skin dividing each nostril. The blunt nose projects beyond the lower jaw in the lake whitefish, which distinguishes this fish from the lake-inhabiting cisco, *Coregonus artedii*, of northeast Alberta (introduced into Lake Minnewanka, Banff) whose lower jaw projects beyond the nose.

Size and Weight

The lake whitefish can grow to 31 in. (80 cm) and weigh up to 22 lbs. (11 kg). However, in the mountain parks, these sizes are rarely reached.

Distribution

The lake whitefish is widespread in Canada in lakes and large rivers. They can potentially be found in all of the mountain parks. However, they are only native to the Athabasca and Waterton drainages within the mountain parks.

Life History

As with all whitefish, they are fall or early winter spawners (October-December). There is no redd or nest constructed for the eggs. The female lays 7,000 to 8,000 eggs per pound of her body weight. The eggs are simply scattered over the lake bottom and left to hatch. Due to the cold water temperatures, 32-36°F (0-2°C), the eggs require approximately five months to hatch, usually just when the ice leaves the lakes. The primary food for both the fry and adult fish are bottom-dwelling organisms, including the larval stages of many insects. Plankton is sometimes eaten as well as an occasional small fish.

Angling

Outside the mountain parks, lake whitefish is a very important commercially caught species. The angler can use wet flies or flies with weighted heads. Small lures and jigs are popularly used through the ice. The mouth of the lake whitefish is soft and tender and care must be taken to not tear the flesh when playing the fish.

These fish move inshore and into tributaries in the fall, while at other times they tend to be widely distributed throughout lakes and larger rivers, often well away from the shore. The young of the year tend to occupy the warmer, more productive water near the surface and near shore, and are often visible at ice-free margins in larger numbers. As summer progresses, they move offshore.

The dorsal fin of a lake whitefish is dark and pointed, while the dorsal fin of the mountain whitefish is grey or dusky. This female lake whitefish, stomach bulging with eggs, was a river-caught individual from a deep hole of slow to moderate current. ➤

Wayne Roberts

Lake **Whitefish**

85

Pygmy whitefish (above) may easily be overlooked among young lake whitefish (below) or mountain whitefish.

The Kakwa River, near Willmore Wilderness Park, is an excellent river for mountain whitefish.

11. Mountain Whitefish *Prosopium williamsoni*, with reference to the pygmy whitefish, *Prosopium coulteri*

Family Name: Salmonidae

Other Names: Rocky Mountain whitefish. Grayling is a common name used by some fishermen in the Banff vicinity. This should not be confused with the arctic grayling.

Description

The mountain whitefish is a round-headed, round-bodied silvery fish with a large adipose fin. The mouth is slightly subterminal (the lower jaw being behind the front of the head) without teeth in the jaws, and the snout is somewhat pointed. The dorsal surfaces and fins are light brown while the sides and belly are silver and white. The lower jaw is short and blunt. Each nostril is divided by a single flap (lake whitefish have a double flap in each nostril). Young possess parr marks (dark vertical or round blotches along the sides) typical of many salmonids. Young lake whitefish lack parr marks.

There is another species of uncommon whitefish sometimes caught by anglers in Jasper and Waterton Lakes National Parks, and easily confused with young mountain whitefish. This is the diminutive pygmy whitefish, *Prosopium coulteri*, a species with a highly scattered and disjunct distribution primarily in northwestern North America. Rarely more than six in. (15 cm) in length, the tiny pygmy whitefish is distinguished from a young mountain whitefish by its rounded head and its large scales which number less than 70 along its lateral line (mountain whitefish count from 75-90). Its small adipose fin (a small fleshy fin on the back behind the dorsal fin) has a base shorter than the length of the fish's eye (mountain whitefish have a large adipose fin longer at its base than the length of its eye). The head of a pygmy whitefish is more blunt in shape than the pointed snout of the mountain whitefish. Look over your small whitefish when you catch one, you may just meet the pygmy whitefish. This fish is not known to occur in Banff National Park, although the authors suspect it may be discovered there. If you find a pygmy whitefish in Banff, report your discovery to park officials.

*This riffle pool in the upper Red Deer River is a typical holding
area for mountain whitefish.*

*The bulbous "bottle-nosed" snout is typical of the mountain
whitefish.*

*The large adipose fin and the cylindrical shape of the body are
characteristic of mountain whitefish.* ➤

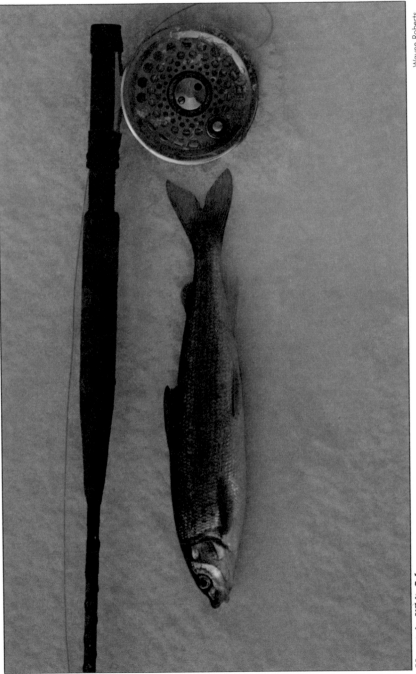

Mountain Whitefish

Size and Weight

Mountain whitefish can grow to 20 in. (50 cm) and weigh up to 4.4 lbs. (2 kg). In a practical sense, the fish rarely attain this size; 14 in. (35 cm) and 2.2 lbs. (1 kg) is to be expected.

Distribution

The mountain whitefish can be found throughout the mountain parks. Generally, they are widely distributed on both sides of the Continental Divide with many streams, rivers, and lakes supporting large numbers of this species.

Life History

The mountain whitefish is a late fall (October-December) spawner. No redd or nest for the eggs is constructed as occurs with trout and charr. The female may lay 2,000 to 9,000 eggs, depending on her size. Since the eggs are spawned when the water temperature is cold and getting colder, 35°F (2°C), the incubation period is quite long; eggs hatch in about five months, March to April. The primary foods of both the young and adults are bottom-dwelling fauna (animal organisms), but also include terrestrial insects; occasionally they may eat other small fish.

Angling

Mountain whitefish are excellent sport fish which may be caught with small dry or wet flies or hooks baited with stonefly larvae, maggots, or fish eggs. Anglers must be very careful when playing these fish as they possess soft mouths which tear or rip easily. Light tackle and fly rods are recommended.

Fishing for mountain whitefish may be relatively hit-and-miss due to the fish's vagrant nature. Schools containing aggregations of similar size fish will make feeding excursions into tributaries in mid-summer then return to the main river to spawn in the fall. Late summer offers the best fishing due to the concentrations of larger fish for spawning purposes. Aggregations will follow a stream course during any season, foraging and then moving onward to a fresh foraging location. A pool absolutely full of fish may on another day be virtually empty.

12. Burbot *Lota lota*

Family Name: Gadidae, codfish family

Other Names: ling, freshwater ling or cod, lawyer, eelpoint, and cusk

Description

The burbot, as can be seen from the photos, is a highly distinctive fish with an elongated body that is dark to olive-brown on the dorsal (back) surfaces with darkened irregular markings. The ventral (belly) surface is light yellow to dusky-brown in color. One easily identifiable characteristic is that it has two dorsal fins, with the second one being at least half the length of the body. The anal fin is equally elongated. The scales are very small and hard to see. The head is flattened, and there is a single barbel, a long slender worm-like probe, under the front of the lower jaw.

Size and Weight

Maximum lengths may be up to 39.5 in. (one meter) with body weights up to 14.3 lbs. (6.5 kg).

Distribution

The burbot is found along the entire eastern drainages of the Rocky Mountains from Alaska into Montana, although it may occur in many of the major rivers and some lakes on both sides of the Continental Divide.

Life History

The burbot can inhabit a wide range of habitats from deep cold-water lakes to small headwater streams. Typically, spawning takes place in the winter under the ice, from January to early April. Females can produce eggs when three years old. Eggs are spawned in shallow waters and are scattered over the bottom. Burbot produce great numbers of eggs: it is not uncommon for large burbot to spawn up to 1,000,000 eggs each year. The eggs take 30 days or more for incubation to occur. For burbot, and indeed for all other species, the development time for the eggs is extended by cold water temperatures.

Stan Clements

The single barbel on the chin and the elongated tips of the pelvic fin are important tactile features for burbot.

Burbot are principally nocturnal. The single barbel is a chemically sensitive and tactile device held straight out while foraging. With the extended barbel probing beneath rocks and debris, they can be effective predators. In some streams they eat a considerable number of sculpins and leopard frogs. The barbel and the elongated tips of the pelvic fins are adaptations for feeding in low light conditions. Bottom-dwelling organisms, fish eggs, small fish and dead organisms provide the majority of the diet. Aquatic insects or invertebrates are the principal diet of small burbot, with fish becoming more important as the burbot becomes larger. As an historical note, at one time the tough skin was used in Siberia in place of glass for windows.

Angling

Since burbot are most active at night, daytime fishing may often prove unsuccessful. Ice fishing may show better results. The photo demonstrates that burbot will even on occasion strike a wet fly.

Burbot show a wide variation in color. This individual, caught on a wet fly, was 17 in. (43.2 cm) in length, and possibly four years of age.

►

Burbot

As burbot tend to avoid bright light, and mountain waters are usually highly transparent, they remain under cover or occupy dimly lit depths. Young of the year are often seen in shallow water in broad daylight. Adults congregate in February-March in shallow water in lakes, and at such times large numbers may be caught.

Professor Butler on horseback to a high lake fishing location in the Tonquin Valley. Horses are a convenient access vehicle into many roadless areas of the mountain parks, and there are numerous outfitters available which cater to angling opportunities.

13. Northern Pike *Esox lucius*

Family Name: Esocidae

Other Names: Pike, jackfish

Description

The northern pike is an elongated fish with the body laterally (side-to-side) compressed. The bottom jaw is prominent, and there are several rows of sharp teeth in the roof of the mouth. There are several color phases, from olive to brownish-green to medium grey. At times, the fins may appear dark brown. The dorsal fin is situated well back on the body just ahead of the caudal peduncle (the fleshy end of the body behind the anal fin and before the caudal or tail fin), an adaptation which permits a stealthy approach combined with a darting thrust. Juvenile pike tend to have light vertical bars on their sides near the tail. Light spots all over are an adult characteristic. "Silver pike," a color mutant, lack the light vertical bars or spots.

Size and Weight

The northern pike may be up to 42 in. (1.2 meters) long and weigh 44 lbs. (20 kg). Invariably almost all large pike are females, as growth in males slows quickly when they become sexually mature.

Distribution

The northern pike is circumpolar (occurring around the earth in the northern regions) and is found in almost all the drainages in Alberta; however, there is limited distribution in the mountain parks. Talbot Lake, Jasper is a notable location for pike, and they are common in many foothills lakes.

Jim Butler

Northern pike are not common in the mountain parks. This habitat in Jasper National Park, with an elk in the foreground, is one of the few places suitable for them. Emergent vegetation is an essential habitat feature.

Life History

Since pike prefer clear, warm, slow-moving aquatic habitats with emergent vegetation, they rarely occur in high mountain lakes. They favour weedy areas that provide cover and food in the form of aquatic insects, invertebrates and smaller fish. Forage fish which commonly frequent weedy lake margins include pearl dace and fine-scaled dace, fathead minnows, lake chubs, brook sticklebacks and suckers. Pike have been known to eat ducklings and even small muskrats. While they are well adapted to eat large prey, they are conservative predators, often going for long periods between meals. Spawning takes place in the spring just after the ice breaks up. The eggs are deposited over vegetation in shallow areas along lakeshores or in tributaries. The eggs hatch quickly

Fly-fishing for northern pike is greatly increasing in popularity. This individual shows the adult pattern of light spots all over. Juveniles tend to have light vertical bars. ➤

96

Wayne Roberts

Northern Pike

as the water warms. Where suckers occur, their eggs often hatch two weeks after the pike, providing a highly important forage food for pike through their first year. Some fast-growing young pike may be 8-11 in. (20-28 cm) long by late fall.

Angling

The northern pike is a very popular game fish both because of its size and easy catchability. Since these fish are territorial or sedentary and prefer the shallow shore areas, they can be stalked and approached. Large pike in the shallows during spring are likely to be pre-spawning females and should be enjoyed by observing only, and certainly never removed. Pike readily feed during the daytime and respond well to lures and spoons. Fly-fishing for pike using wet flies containing yellows and reds is increasingly popular. Dry-fly mouse imitations are also used with a high level of success. With light fly tackle even small pike provide excellent sport, and the single hook is less likely to harm the fish for its release.

In spring pike are accessible while they move into tributaries and flooded lake margins. Otherwise they spend much of the time resting and moving cautiously through shallow to moderate depths. The vicinity of tributaries is a preferred site. They are relatively scarce in deep, open water.

14. White Sucker *Catostomus commersoni,* with reference to the largescale sucker, *Catostomus macrocheilus*

Family Name: Catostomidae

Other Names: common sucker

Description

There are only four different suckers to be encountered along the east and west slopes of the Canadian Rockies. They are easily separated into two groups depending on whether the scales are large or small. The white sucker and largescale sucker each have large conspicuous scales which can easily be counted (there should be less than 80) with the unaided eye along the length of the lateral line (a series of pore-like openings that appear as a broken line along the length of the fish). The longnose sucker and mountain sucker are both "fine-scale" suckers with scales difficult to count with the unaided eye, although in both, the scales become conspicuously larger near the tail.

The largescale sucker is principally a British Columbia species, occurring rarely in Yoho and Kootenay National Parks and ranging into Alberta only north of Jasper National Park along the upper Peace River. It is easily separated from the other three suckers in that it has a longer dorsal fin containing 14-16 dorsal rays (all others have 10-12 dorsal rays) as well as possessing a conspicuously narrow caudal peduncle. The white sucker (the other sucker with large scales) has a stout (larger) caudal peduncle.

The mouth of the large-scale white sucker is moderate in size and is located only slightly below the rounded snout. There are small fleshy projections or ridges (papillae) on the lower lip, with a deep separation or cleft at the midline which extends all the way to the mouth. The other suckers have the cleft stopping just short of the mouth (see photograph in mountain sucker section). The only other large-scale sucker of the Canadian Rockies is the rarely found largescale sucker, *C. macrocheilus*

Coloration in the white sucker is blackish to grey dorsally (back), shading to silver laterally (sides) and ventrally (belly area). The ventral

Suckers can be divided for the purpose of recognition into those with large scales and those with fine scales. The white sucker (top) has large conspicuous scales, while the longnose sucker (bottom) has small scales difficult to count with the unaided eye. Note that both individuals are mature males, as made evident by the spawning tubercles (pimple-like projections) on their tail and anal fins.

surface is white to cream colored with all fins being dark. The sex of ripe adult suckers can usually be distinguished by the presence of tubercles (a soft or hardened lump or projection on the surface) on the tails and anal fins of males. An examination of the pelvic fin of males will show that the inner (inside or next to the body) rays are as long as those on the outer edge. On female suckers the longest rays of the pelvic fin are on the outside.

Size and Weight

White suckers can grow to 20 in. (50 cm) and weigh up to 4.4 lbs. (2 kg).

White suckers are often found in pools along mountain streams. Note the thick caudal peduncle on this large scaled species. ➤

White Sucker

Distribution

The common or white sucker, like the longnose sucker, is widely distributed. In Alberta, Montana and British Columbia it inhabits most major drainages, especially large rivers and moderate to large lakes.

Life History

The white sucker feeds on the bottom of streams and lakes, consuming insect larvae, freshwater clams or mollusks and small plants. Spawning takes place immediately following ice break-up, in the shallows of creeks, rivers, or along lake shores. There is no parental protection of the spawning location or care of the young that hatch about two weeks after spawning. As fry and shortly thereafter, the mouth is terminal (at the foreward end of the head), and they feed near the surface on small aquatic plants or plankton. As the fish matures, the mouth becomes more ventral (on the underside of the head) and they feed principally by sucking invertebrates from the underwater or substrate surfaces. Like the longnose and mountain suckers, this sucker is an important food source for trout and pike and provides a valuable service by consuming diseased, dead, or otherwise unviable trout eggs, thus reducing the chance of disease or fungus spreading to healthy eggs.

Angling

Although the white sucker is not an important game fish, it is caught by anglers and it plays an important role in the food chain. Again, young white suckers are a primary source of food for other fish and "fishermen" in the environment.

Bob Purdy

Largescale suckers have a very narrow caudal peduncle and a long dorsal fin.

15. Longnose Sucker *Catostomus catostomus*

Family Name: Catostomidae

Description

The name longnose is derived from the fact that the head has a rounded snout which overhangs the mouth. This "fine-scale" sucker has fleshy rounded lips without a notch separating the upper from lower lip (see photograph in mountain sucker section). The lower lip is cleft, often completely split. The dorsal surfaces are dark olive-green to brown with the ventral surfaces being white to cream colored. In breeding color, the males become conspicuously red and black, puzzling sportsmen unfamiliar with this large and striking fish.

Size and Weight

The longnose sucker can be up to 25 in. (64 cm) in length and weigh up to 7 lbs. (3.25 kg). They are much larger than the mountain suckers.

Distribution

The longnose sucker is widely distributed throughout North America and Siberia. It is the only sucker that inhabits arctic environments, and is therefore common throughout the mountain parks.

Life History

The longnose sucker prefers large deep lakes and reservoirs although it can be found in rivers and streams, and in deep waters with lake whitefish and lake trout. They are bottom-dwellers feeding on small animals such as freshwater clams or mollusks, freshwater shrimp or crustaceans and insect larvae. Spawning occurs early in the spring in shallow riffles, where streams feed into lakes. The female may lay up to 30,000 eggs, which it scatters over the substrate without benefit of a nest. The longnose sucker may hybridize with both mountain and white suckers. Longnose suckers seem to live to exceptional old ages in the mountain parks, a result of cold water slowing the fish's metabolism. One female taken from Dog Lake in Kootenay National Park proved to be at least 31 years old when caught. This was ten years older than the previously known longevity record for the species.

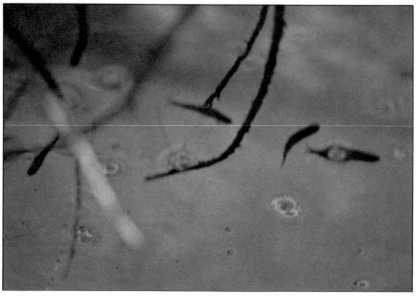

Young trout fingerlings, such as these, find newly hatched suckers an important food source. Suckers often hatch two weeks after pike, making them an important pike food source as well.

Angling

The longnose sucker can be an exciting and challenging sport fish, most frequently encountered in streams during spring spawning runs. It is the most athletic of the suckers, a heavy fish and a strong fighter, very rarely experienced by traditional anglers. It is a fish readily available and well suited to the fly fishermen in search of a novel and innovative spring challenge.

Spawning male longnose suckers can be very attractive. This one, caught on a bucktail during a spring spawning run, offered exceptional sport and an innovative challenge. ➤

Longnose Sucker

16. Mountain Sucker *Catostumus platyrhynchus*

Family Name: Catostomidae

Other Names: flatnose or mudsucker

Description

The mountain sucker is one of two sucker species found in the mountain parks that are covered with small inconspicuous scales (except for the unscaled tail).

The two "fine-scale" suckers can be distinguished by their lips. The longnose sucker has large fleshy rounded lips without a notch separating the lower lip from the upper lip. The longnose sucker has a conspicuously large anal fin which the mountain sucker lacks. The mountain sucker may be distinguished from other suckers by a notch on each side of the mouth where the lips meet. The fine-scale mountain sucker has a dorsal (back) surface that varies from moss-green to dark brown, often mottled, while the ventral (belly) surface is white or cream coloured. It often has several dark saddles over the back, facilitating immediate recognition of the species when in the water.

Size and Weight

The mountain sucker is a small sucker, generally reaching a total length of less than eight inches (20 cm) with weight less than 9 oz. (0.25 kg).

Distribution

The mountain sucker occurs in the drainages of the South and North Saskatchewan Rivers in Alberta and the North Thompson River in British Columbia. It also occurs in isolated populations from Alberta to Utah and Colorado.

Life History

Since mountain suckers prefer the cold, clear water of creeks and rivers with gravel, sand and boulders, they are rarely found in lakes. Spawning takes place in late spring or early summer when the water temperature is in the 51-66°F (11-19°C) range. The actual spawning is over gravel or rubble bottoms.

Angling

Mountain suckers are not angled for as sport fish. However, they are occasionally caught and therefore do comprise part of the angler's catch in our mountain parks. Because of their size and abundance they are an important source of food, especially for trout and "other fishermen" in the environment. Like other suckers, and birds such as dippers and mergansers, their scavenging of spawning areas for dead eggs (which soon collect fungus that spreads to live eggs) gives them an important clean-up role in the trout environment.

Waterton Lakes National Park

American Dipper

Dippers, as well as suckers play an important role in consuming dead trout eggs, reducing the chance of fungus spreading to viable eggs.

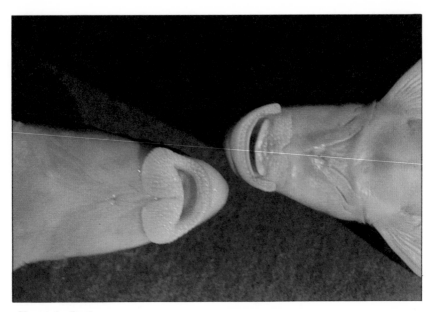

Mountain Sucker   Wayne Roberts

The mouths of suckers are useful for identification. In separating the two "fine-scaled" suckers, note that the fleshy rounded lips of the longnose sucker (left) lack the notch on each side of the mouth where the lips meet. This notch is evident on the mouth of the mountain sucker (right). Note also the pronounced cleft in the lower lip of the longnose.

An angler wisely maintains a low
profile at a beaver dam. Beaver
dams are always a mixed blessing.
Dams such as this provide essential
overwintering areas for mountain
whitefish, brook trout, rainbow trout,
brown trout, cutthroat, and bull
trout. But they also flood spawning
riffles and reduce oxygen levels.

Frank de Boon

Frank de Boon

Habitats such as this offer good
holding water and over-wintering
areas below the plunge pool. Gravel
areas are washed and built-up by
the turbulence below and along side
the plunge pool, and these gravel
deposits are often important
spawning beds for trout and charr.
Sometimes only a few such
spawning beds are available for
miles.

Lake outlets such as this at Lake
O'Hara, Yoho, are important
spawning and rearing areas for trout.
Zooplankton, normally scattered
throughout a wide area of the lake
such as the copepod, Diaptomus, are
funneled by the current through these
constricted areas. Strategically
located trout lay in wait to forage
with relatively low expenditures of
energy.

David Donald

Snow-fed streams like this, while common, are cold and have very low productivity. Many such headwater tributaries dry up by August when the snow melts. Temporary invasion of such places does occur by small yearling trout, when at times of highest numbers they disperse to fill all available niches.

David Donald

Sandra Gibbon

Waterfalls such as this can prove to be a barrier to upstream dispersal, but more for fall spawners such as charr, in periods of low water. Spring spawners such as cutthroats and rainbows can navigate falls such as this at spring high water levels.

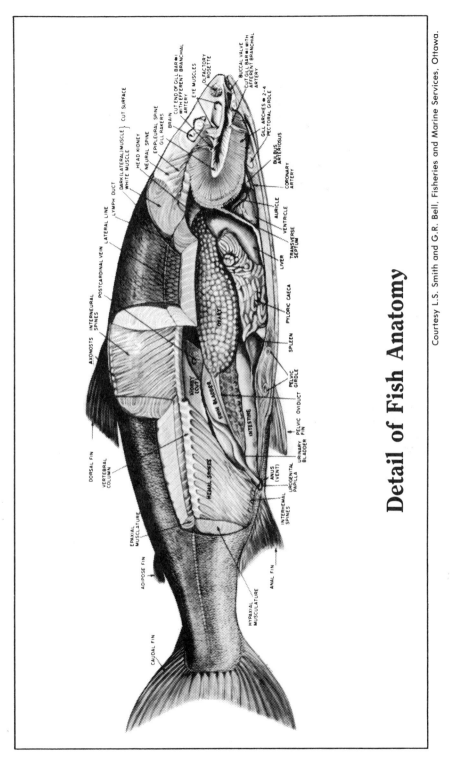

Detail of Fish Anatomy

Courtesy L.S. Smith and G.R. Bell, Fisheries and Marine Services, Ottawa.

Labels (clockwise from top):

CUT END OF GILL BAR — WITH EFFERENT BRANCHIAL ARTERY
BRAIN
OLFACTORY ROSETTE
BUCCAL VALVE
CUT GILL BAR — WITH AFFERENT BRANCHIAL ARTERY
GILL ARCHES — 2-4
PECTORAL GIRDLE
BULBUS ARTERIOSUS
CORONARY ARTERY
AURICLE
VENTRICLE
LIVER
TRANSVERSE SEPTUM
PYLORIC CAECA
SPLEEN
PELVIC GIRDLE
PELVIC OVIDUCT
PELVIC FIN
URINARY BLADDER
UROGENITAL PAPILLA
ANUS (VENT)
INTERHEMAL SPINES
HYPAXIAL MUSCULATURE
ANAL FIN
CAUDAL FIN
ADIPOSE FIN
EPAXIAL MUSCLATURE
VERTEBRAL COLUMN
DORSAL FIN
AXONOSTS
INTERNEURAL SPINES
POSTCARDINAL VEIN
LATERAL LINE
LYMPH DUCT
DARK (LATERAL) MUSCLE } CUT SURFACE
WHITE MUSCLE
HEAD KIDNEY
NEURAL SPINE
EPIPLEURAL SPINE
GILL RAKERS
EYE MUSCLES
OVARY
KIDNEY (CUT)
SWIM BLADDER
INTESTINE
HEMAL SPINES

111

An adult bull trout of this size is a product of at least ten years of growth, and the reproductive potential of such fish is important in the maintenance of fishery stocks. The angler who released this fish was rewarded the following morning by catching the same fish again.

CATCHING AND RELEASING

Catch-and-release is nothing new to the sport of angling. In fact, ethical anglers have been voluntarily practicing sound conservation behavior for decades. Such actions have been endorsed by Roderick Haig-Brown, Lee Wulff and many other angler-writers over the past fifty years. While their audience is growing, so too are the overall numbers of anglers. Fishery stocks have been shrinking as a direct result.

Through proper release techniques, you can greatly enhance the survival chances of your fish. Catch-and-release regulations are just one in the broad array of management tools available to fishery managers. Mandatory catch-and-release regulations also usually incorporate restrictions on the type of tackle allowed for the protection of selected wild trout populations. However, many sportsmen voluntarily practice catch-and-release on all waters and all species.

Whether you are releasing an undersized or a mature fish, a big trout you caught just for sport, or are concerned about maintaining future spawning stocks in the park, here are six basic guidelines for releasing your fish.

1. Play and release the fish as quickly and efficiently as possible. By avoiding playing a fish for a long time you will leave it with enough energy to recover. Over-exhaustion and undue stress are often the causes of fish dying upon release. Ironically, what to the angler is a great thrill is to the fish a matter of life and death.

2. Try to leave the fish in the water at all times! The water provides oxygen and serves as a cradle to protect the fish from injury due to improper handling.

3. Keep fingers and all other items out of the gills. Fish gills, like your lungs, serve to provide needed oxygen and are quite fragile. If the fish is struggling vigorously, you can avoid holding the fish in the gill area by turning it over and supporting the fish on its back in the water. This also calms the fish.

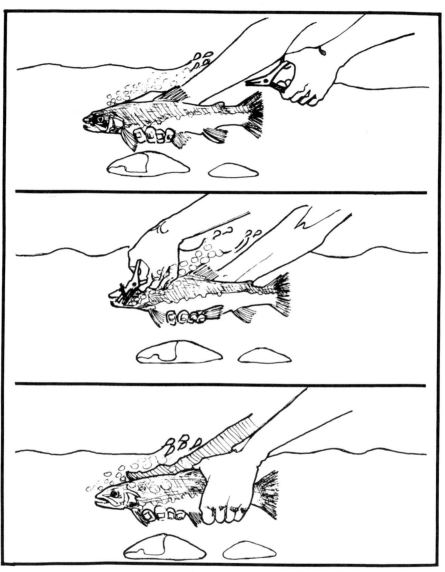

Employ proper catch-and-release techniques to minimize the possibility of harming the fish. Handle the fish gently from below, keeping it submerged. Carefully remove the hook with needlenose pliers or surgical hemostat. (De-barbed hooks facilitate removal.) After removing the hook, resuscitate the fish by moving it back and forth, facing upstream to help move the oxygen-rich water through the fish's gills.

4. Handle the fish gently. Never grab or squeeze a fish as internal organs may be easily damaged. The less touching and grasping the better, since both scales and the mucous body-coating protect against bacterial and fungal infections. The loss of any of these disease defences may be serious.

5. Be especially careful when removing the hooks! Too often hooks are torn out by unthinking anglers and fish easily die from such abuse. Avoid treble hooks or double hooks; they do far too much damage. For fish hooked in the mouth, use a pair of long-nosed pliers or a medical hemostat to minimize de-hooking injuries. Serious damage occurs when the fish swallows the hook, but this can usually be avoided by not using baited hooks. If the hook is swallowed, or caught in the eye or gill, simply cut the leader and release the fish. The hook will dissolve away in a short time. Hooks of stainless steel or brass will not dissolve away, and when left in a released fish, may infect or poison the fish. Check to see whether your hooks are made of such metals and avoid using them. Debarb hooks in advance by squeezing down the barb with pliers. This also greatly simplifies hook removal. (The barb on a hook is far less essential in landing a fish than most realize.) Once a fish begins bleeding from the gills or surrounding delicate membranes it will almost always die, so be careful.

6. When the fish is ready to swim away on its own you no longer need to support it. If the fish is fatigued, cradle the fish with its head in an upstream position and move it gently back and forth to stimulate artifical resuscitation. Support the fish gently by holding the tail with one hand and cupping your other hand under the belly.

National parks are not locations to seek out fish to fill your freezer. Keep only the fish required for that occasional campfire dinner, and even then be moderate. Large, spawning-age fish should be allowed to spawn. In contrast to the old tradition of keeping the big ones and releasing the small ones, if you choose to eat fish, select from the many younger fish and dispatch your choice quickly and humanely with a sharp blow on the head. Don't leave fish gasping to die on the bank or in the bottom of the canoe.

All anglers should know how to properly release a fish regardless of their orientation toward the sport. Studies have shown that the same fish can be caught several times, if only released properly. Be aware of, and take interest in releasing fish properly. Your and our future fishing

Roland Maw

Releasing a small arctic grayling. Grayling are susceptible to overfishing and so should be protected by catch-and-release.

opportunities in the mountain national parks depend upon knowledgeable and informed anglers.

Sport fishing in our mountain parks is a unique opportunity to be cherished for its overall experience. We have a great source of sport fish in our mountain parks; that is a quality source and not a quantity source of fish. Extensive biological research has shown that mountain species are slow to grow, and that means slow to mature and spawn. Food sources are not as plentiful, water temperatures are colder, natural phenomena such as floods are frequent and many other forms of wildlife are also dependent on the same fishery stocks. Anglers compete for a limited resource now, and the competition will increase as the popularity of angling increases.

The fish you release you will likely never see again, but someone else certainly may. You may one day meet one of the offspring, or recall before a crackling fireplace the recollection of that fish, its setting, and the circumstances of its catch. While the fish may still swim free and continue to spawn, it will always be more vividly saved in the mind's eye and the depth of the heart.

FISHING, FISH
. . . AND BEARS

The story is told of a fly fisherman who was casting for rainbows in a favorite stream. As he stood in the knee-high grass just below a favorite pool, he made a back-cast preparing for a new presentation. The line suddenly went taut. Thinking the willows the source of his torment, he looked over his shoulder to see what he had caught. There sat a black bear, on his haunches, pawing at the imitation mosquito caught in his ear. Not a recommended bear-catching technique for either hunter or fisherman. As both grizzly and black bears are commonly encountered by anglers in the mountain parks, the authors feel that a few additional words are warranted on the subject.

Anglers are cautioned about the following:

First: Obtain, read and follow the instructions in the Parks Canada or other official government publications on bears. Do not go looking for trouble by approaching a bear. This is especially true for grizzlies and sows with cubs. The sow will defend herself and the cubs.

Second: Keep a clean camp and fishing site. Any baits used, fish caught, or just the smell of fish on clothes or equipment may be enough to cause a bear to look for food. Foods like fish, bacon and meats all have heavy lingering odors. When cooking fish or other foods, always cook away from your sleeping area. Store food at least 100 meters away from your sleeping area, day and night. Use approved fish storage facilities if available.

All fish, fish entrails and garbage should be sealed in plastic bags and packed out of the fishing area. This is an important courtesy to other people who may choose to use the area after you. After all, you may want to return to the area yourself.

Third: Avoid surprising bears. They do not take surprises very well. When walking along streams, or in areas of poor visibility, make some noise. This will warn the bears of your presence and give them time to move away.

Grizzly bear

Black bear

Last: If you encounter a bear or a bear approaches you, stay calm—do not panic. Do not run, as the bear can easily catch you if it so desires. Move away slowly. There is no need to further excite the bear. If the bear is unaware of your presence, as indicated by a lack of reaction, make some noise. The bear should begin to move away. If the bear begins to approach, begin a retreat. If the bear continues to advance, lay something like a coat, hat, your fishing gear or day-pack on the ground. This may delay the bear long enough for you to get further away. If further advances are made, move toward cover and, if possible, climb a tree. If you are with other people, always try to stay together or get into groups.

Even though you may do everything as indicated here and in the pamphlets, there are no guarantees. Whenever you enter bear-occupied habitats, there is a possibility of encountering a bear. It is their environment here, and you are the visitor. The sight of their tracks on the shoreline, like the call of a loon or the howl of the wolf, is a testimony to the area's wildness. Like the wild, native-spawned trout you seek, may it always remain that way.

ABOUT THE AUTHORS

James R. Butler is a professor of Parks and Wildlife in the Forest Science Department of the University of Alberta, Edmonton. Dr. Butler teaches courses in parks and nature interpretation, including a course in Forest Wildlife which teaches the identification and ecology of native fishes. He also conducts research on sport fisherman attitudes and satisfactions. An avid fly-fisherman and member of Trout Unlimited, Dr. Butler has travelled widely to fish for trout, salmon, bonefish and other sport fish.

Dr. Butler, with his faithful labrador "Prince," casts for brown trout on the famous Au Sable River, Michigan.

Roland R. Maw is a professor of Parks and Wildland Management in the Environmental Science Department of the Lethbridge Community College. Mr. Maw teaches courses in park operations and park management which include policy and operational strategies for the conservation of natural resources. He lived for several years near Yellowstone National Park, and as an avid fly-fisherman has travelled throughout North America to fish for salmon, trout, charr and other sport fish.

Professor Maw holds a large Chinook salmon he caught while angling in Alaska.

Index

Rainbow trout are one of the most popular sportfish in Western Canada.

Jim Butler